THE SUPREMACISTS

Also by Phyllis Schlafly

THE SUPREMACISTS

*The Tyranny of Judges
and How to Stop It*

PHYLLIS SCHLAFLY

SPENCE PUBLISHING COMPANY • DALLAS
2004

Published in the United States by
Spence Publishing Company
111 Cole Street
Dallas, Texas 75207

ISBN: 1-890626-65-1 (pbk.)
978-1-890626-65-5

Library of Congress Control Number
for the hardcover edition: 2004107716

Printed in the United States of America

Contents

"We will not stand for judges who undermine democracy by legislating from the bench and try to remake the culture of America by court order."

PRESIDENT GEORGE W. BUSH
March 8, 2004, Dallas

Foreword

WHAT IS THE FUTURE of self-government in America? Will we continue to be the world's greatest self-governing people, a land of liberty and of the prosperity that flows from freedom?

Or will we, like so many others, allow ourselves to be ruled by a small band of elitists who pretend to be wiser than the rest of us and force their policies upon us?

Our American institutions and culture are being undermined today by judicial supremacists. They are carrying out a revolution in our system of government, and most Americans don't realize it because it has happened stealthily and sporadically over the last fifty years. Activist judges have been legislating a liberal agenda that opposes religious values, conventional morality, the Constitution, and even the right of American citizens to govern ourselves.

A supremacist is one who believes in or advocates the supremacy of a particular group. The threat to America comes precisely from those who believe in and advocate the supremacy of one particular group—judges—over the lawful wishes of the people.

Textbooks still say that we have three balanced branches of government—but textbooks are badly behind the times because one branch has assumed authority over the other two. Today, we are suffering from the oppressive rule of judicial supremacists who have replaced the rule of law with the rule of judges.

We respect the proper role of judges. We need judges, and we need a properly functioning judicial branch. We need judges for the same reason that baseball needs umpires. Someone has to call the balls and strikes and resolve close plays. But umpires are never allowed to change the rules of the game. We would not tolerate an umpire who called a batter out after two strikes. As Chief Justice John G. Roberts Jr. said in his confirmation hearings, "I will remember that it's my job to call balls and strikes and not to pitch or bat."

The assault by the judicial supremacists against the Constitution and the rule of law is the most serious issue facing our political system today. If unchecked, judicial supremacy will continue to grow like a cancer and destroy our republic.

This book describes what judges have done to our nation and explains how the Constitution contains all the tools needed to rescue America from the tyranny of judges.

THE SUPREMACISTS

Judges Rewrite the Constitution

T HE UNITED STATES CONSTITUTION did not create judicial supremacy or consign us to be ruled by a judicial oligarchy. On the contrary, the Constitution separated the vast powers of the federal government into three branches—legislative, executive, and judicial—with an ingenious system of checks and balances so that each branch can serve as a continuing check on the others. We call this the separation of powers, and our state governments are also modeled on the same design. James Madison wrote in *Federalist 51* that this system is the best way to achieve the twin goals of liberty and justice. By "so contriving the interior structure of the government," Madison wrote, "its several constituent parts may, by their mutual relations, be the means of keeping each other in their proper places."

But Congress, the legal establishment, and the American people have all failed in their duty to keep the judiciary in its proper place.

The unique and brilliant design of our Constitution —the system of checks and balances, with each branch checking the power of the other two branches—has been replaced by the Imperial Judiciary. Judicial supremacists have grabbed unconstitutional powers for the courts, and Congress has failed to restrain their power grab.

Our Constitution's Framers designed the judicial branch to be the least powerful of the three branches. Alexander Hamilton wrote in *Federalist 78* that the judiciary "will always be the least dangerous" branch of government because it has the least capacity to "annoy or injure" our constitutional rights. His prediction was correct for a century and a half, but today the judiciary annoys and injures our constitutional rights to a shocking extent.

The U.S. Constitution vests "all" legislative powers in the Congress. That means no legislative powers are granted to the courts. Yet, over the past fifty years, judges have become increasingly activist—legislating from the bench, and writing their own policies and attitudes into the law. In the latter half of the twentieth century, some of our most far-reaching social, economic and political decisions have been made by judges rather than by our elected representatives.

Judicial supremacists have:

- censored the Pledge of Allegiance in public schools
- removed the Ten Commandments from public schools, buildings, and parks
- changed the definition of marriage

- banned the acknowledgment of God in public schools, at graduations, and at football games
- imposed taxes and spending of taxpayers' money
- rewritten laws of criminal procedures
- dismantled laws that protect internal security
- imposed the social experimentation called forced school busing
- upheld racial preferences and quotas in hiring and college admissions
- outlawed term limits for Members of Congress
- rewritten laws on the conduct of elections
- banned the Boy Scouts from public property

Judicial supremacists have invented so-called rights such as:

- the right to abortion
- the right to same-sex marriage licenses
- the right to show and publish pornography, even with taxpayers' money
- the right of illegal aliens to receive taxpayer-paid benefits

Judicial supremacists have arbitrarily overturned laws adopted by majorities in statewide referenda in:

- Arizona
- Arkansas
- California
- Colorado
- Nebraska
- Washington State

Judicial supremacists have set themselves up as a super-executive and grabbed authority to micromanage:

- schools
- prisons
- hiring standards
- legislative reapportionment

THE PROPER ROLES

Social, economic, and political policies should be made by our elected representatives, not by judges. The American people should not allow judges to usurp the constitutional role of legislators. Judges have assumed authorities and responsibilities that the Constitution never gave them, and they are doing great harm—to our society, our culture, our institutions, our schoolchildren, and our right of self-government. We must not permit a judicial oligarchy to rule unchallenged.

We need trial judges to resolve disputes based on applicable law. We want decisions reviewed by appellate courts to ascertain that the law was properly applied. But we do *not* want judges making new law, setting policies, usurping the authority of other branches of government, or imposing their own social and political views on our people. We do *not* want judges rewriting the Constitution under the pretense that they are interpreting it. Article V of the Constitution provides a procedure for amending it, and the judiciary has *no* part in that process.

It is not fashionable to question the authority of the courts. Not recognizing something as wrong for several generations gives it a superficial appearance of being right and allows a noisy clamor to rise in its defense. Those who have profited by the expansion of judicial power have erected formidable barriers against change—and even against criticism.

Our country's future depends on a courageous inquiry into the constitutional errors that have allowed a judicial oligarchy to rule over us. This book will help the American people replace longstanding assumptions and fallacies with the truth. This book offers simple facts, plain reasons, and common sense.

We repeatedly hear the maxim, "We are a nation of laws, not of men." Our Constitution specifically defines *itself*—not the opinions of judges—as "the supreme law of the land." But political judges have turned us into a government of men, not of laws. Judicial grabs for power have been escalating for a half century and there is no end in sight.

One of the "usurpations" that caused Americans to declare our independence in 1776 was royal rulers' "declaring themselves invested with Power to legislate for us in all cases whatsoever." The signers of the Declaration of Independence knew that the essence of freedom is the right to be a self-governing people, to have laws made by representatives whom the voters elect, because government can justly exercise only such powers as are based on "the consent of the governed."

If we are to remain a free and independent nation, we must reject judicial "usurpations," that is, the pretense of judicial supremacists that they are "invested with Power to legislate for us in all cases."

A LIVING AND EVOLVING CONSTITUTION?

The judicial supremacists refuse to be bound by the words and the original understanding of the United States Constitution. Instead, they espouse the theory that the Constitution is a "living" document which can change according to judicially directed "evolution." "Living" and "evolution" (or "evolving") are code words used by judicial supremacists to express their conceit that they can substitute meanings that were never present in the Constitution or our statutes. Activist judges simply ignore the Constitution's plain language and original meaning.

The late Supreme Court Justice William J. Brennan was a leading advocate of these supremacist ideas. In a speech he delivered on November 21, 1982, he argued for "the evolution of constitutional doctrine" and for law itself "to rethink its role." Brennan said that in previous eras "the function of law was to formalize and preserve (accumulated) wisdom," but "over the past 40 years Law has come alive as a living process responsive to changing human needs." He bragged that "evolution of constitutional law has been, in fact, a moving consensus," and that "our constitutional guarantees and the Bill of Rights are tissue paper bastions if they fail to transcend the printed page."

Listen to the arrogance of Brennan's proclamation of judicial supremacy: "The Supreme Court has been, and is, called upon to solve many of the most fundamental issues confronting our democracy, including many upon which our society, consciously or unconsciously, is most deeply divided, and that arouse the deepest emotions. Their resolution, one way or the other, often rewrites our future history."

That is the mindset of liberal elitist judges, who have convinced themselves that *they* should rule over Americans of lesser status. The Constitution does not give judges any authority to evolve or transcend its language. Nobody "called upon" nine life-tenured, unelected, unaccountable justices to solve the fundamental issues confronting us and to dictate our "future history." We must *call upon* our elected representatives to reject these unconstitutional notions.

Another famous liberal Supreme Court activist, the late Justice William O. Douglas, called the Due Process Clause in the U.S. Constitution "the wildcard to be put to such use as the judges choose." In light of Douglas's controversial Las Vegas gambling connections, his metaphor was apt.

The Due Process Clause is included in both the Fifth and Fourteenth Amendments: no person shall be deprived of "life, liberty, or property, without due process of law." That language, which applies, respectively, to the federal government and the states, was clearly intended to ensure that lawful procedures are used by our government. For example, the clause means that accused criminals are entitled to their day in court. The clause was never intended to determine what should or should not be a crime.

The judicial supremacists have used this clause as a wildcard by expanding "due process" to include *substantive rights*. It was used most famously in *Dred Scott v. Sanford* (1857) to expand the rights of slaveowners and in *Roe v. Wade* (1973) to declare a right to abortion. There is no authority in the Constitution for this creative use of the term "due process."

Under "substantive due process," the judicial supremacists assert that the federal courts have the discretion to create new substantive rights not mentioned in the Constitution and to decide what substantive rights should be protected and how extensive that protection should be. Substantive due process has become the fundamental legal theory upon which the judicial activists depend for decisions that have no basis in the Constitution, and it has been cited in more than one hundred Supreme Court decisions since *Roe v. Wade* in 1973.

The attitude of activist justices that they can treat the Constitution like "tissue paper," which they can change by playing a "wildcard," is totally contrary to the intent of the Constitution and must not be tolerated. The trouble with some judges is that once they are appointed to the federal judiciary, they seem to think they have been anointed to rule over the rest of us. They pretend they are *interpreting* the Constitution when in fact they are just writing their own opinions into the law. They selectively choose language to reach preordained conclusions without concern for fidelity to the text, a practice that Harvard law professor Laurence Tribe calls the "free-form" approach.

Americans do not want to live under an Imperial Judiciary. We still adhere to the Constitution, the separation of powers into three branches of government, and the rule of law—and we expect judges to abide by them, too.

The concept of a "living" and "evolving" Constitution has taken root in the political arena. When Al Gore was asked during his 2000 campaign what kind of judges he would appoint, he replied, "I would look for justices of the Supreme Court who understand that our Constitution is a living and breathing document, that it was intended by our founders to be interpreted in the light of the constantly evolving experience of the American people."

This heresy has spread throughout the judicial system. The Massachusetts high court, which mandated the granting of same-sex marriage licenses in *Goodridge v. Department of Public Health* (2003), ruled that "civil marriage is an evolving paradigm." The word "evolving" was used to suggest that there are no enduring standards and that constitutions can be rewritten by power-grabbing judges. The word "paradigm" was used to suggest that the traditional worldview about marriage is temporary and has no rational basis. You know that judges are engaging in activism when they use such code words as "evolving" and "paradigm."

The word "originalist" has come into our national vocabulary to describe judges who base their decisions on the Constitution as written and not on the pretense that the Constitution is evolving. Originalism is not a new idea. As explained by Justice Antonin Scalia in a speech at Vanderbilt University on March 21, 2005, "Originalism was the dominant philosophy until fifty years ago. . . . The Constitution is not a living organism."

Thomas Jefferson was really advocating originalism when he wrote: "On every question of construction, [we should] carry ourselves back to the time when the Constitution was adopted; recollect the spirit manifested in the debates; and instead of trying [to find] what meaning may be squeezed out of the text, or invented against it, conform to the probable one in which it was passed."

Chief Justice John Marshall, expressing the same point of view, wrote in *Marbury v. Madison* that the Constitution has "committed to writing" the limits on the powers of the governmental departments, so that those "limits may not be mistaken or forgotten." To disregard its limits, Marshall wrote, is to "reduce . . . to nothing what we have deemed the greatest improvement on political institutions—a written constitution."

As Justice Scalia told the Vanderbilt students, "Most people think the battle is conservative versus liberals when it's actually originalists versus living constitutionalists."

NEW JUDGES CAN'T SOLVE SUPREMACY PROBLEMS

The federal courts today are precariously balanced between activists who support a radical agenda and constitutionalists who adhere to the Constitution. It is important to elect a President who will appoint only constitutionalist judges—but that alone will not solve the problem because too many judicial supremacists have life tenure, and too many judges become supremacists after they taste judicial power.

President Clinton appointed almost half of all federal judges now serving, and federal judges appointed by Presidents Carter and Johnson are still deciding cases. Presidents Nixon and George H. W. Bush both appointed some activist judges, and a Nixon-appointed judge on the Ninth Circuit (Alfred Goodwin) wrote the infamous Pledge of Allegiance decision in 2002 (*Newdow v. U.S. Congress*).

Seven of the nine justices currently serving on the Supreme Court were appointed by Republican presidents. Someone once asked Dwight Eisenhower if he had made any mistakes as President that he later regretted. Ike replied: Yes, two, and they're both sitting on the Supreme Court.

While the American people typically have the opportunity to correct a bad election result after four years, a bad legal precedent can last for decades or even centuries. Justice William O. Douglas was appointed to the U.S. Supreme Court because President Franklin D. Roosevelt wanted to replace what he called the "nine old men" with young, liberal justices. Douglas stayed on the Court for thirty-six years (writing twelve hundred opinions), through the terms of Presidents Harry Truman, Dwight Eisenhower, John F. Kennedy, Lyndon B. Johnson, Richard Nixon, and Gerald Ford. Douglas's prejudice against religion grew so intense that he even questioned the constitutionality of chaplains in the armed services and the words "In God We Trust" on our money.

When he was a member of Congress, Gerald Ford tried (unsuccessfully) to have Douglas impeached because of his money dealings with Las Vegas gamblers. Four times Justice Douglas took a wife "for better or for worse . . . until death do us part," and he divorced three of his wives. Yet, the American people were locked in a judicial embrace with Douglas no matter how outrageous his decisions or behavior.

Alexander Hamilton wrote in *Federalist 81* that he expected Congress to use its discretion to make appropriate "exceptions and regulations" to keep the judiciary "the least dangerous" of the three branches of government. It's long overdue for Congress to protect us from dangerous judges who are assaulting fundamental American principles.

THE COUP D'ÉTAT

Judge Robert H. Bork describes some of the enormous damage that activist judges have inflicted on America in his book *Coercing Virtue: The Worldwide Rule of Judges*. He finds that the courts are dominated by faux intellectuals of the Left who, unable to persuade the people or the legislatures, "avoid the verdict of the ballot box" by engaging in "politics masquerading as law." We are "increasingly governed not by law or elected representatives, but by unelected, unrepresentative, unaccountable committees of lawyers applying no law other than their own will."

All over the nation, special interest advocacy groups are forum-shopping to find judges willing to bypass the Constitution and write their own social and sexual preferences into the law. Plaintiffs are seeking out judges willing to cooperate in deconstructing our culture by abolishing the Pledge of Allegiance and the Ten Commandments to please the atheists, and by abolishing marriage standards and anti-pornography statutes to induce the nation to condone unrestricted sex.

Judges are not trained to consider the trouble their rulings may cause. When judges rewrite laws regarding social policy, they are generally clueless about the potential consequences. Judges lack the necessary information to make political and social policy decisions, they don't have the political processes to ensure that diverse interests are represented, and they don't hold hearings to assess the damage they might cause.

Americans believe that revolutionaries usually come dressed in military garb, but Judge Bork details how America has suffered a coup d'état by men and women in black robes who have changed the rule of law to the rule of judges. Here is how Justice Antonin Scalia describes what happened: "What secret knowledge, one must wonder, is breathed into lawyers when they become justices of this Court, that enables them to discern that a practice which the text of the Constitution does not clearly proscribe, and which our people have regarded as constitutional for 200 years, is in fact unconstitutional?   . . . Day by day, case by case, [the Court] is busy designing a Constitution for a country I do not recognize."

The cancer of judicial supremacy will not go away until the American people rise up and repudiate it. It's time for the American people to notify their elected representatives, federal and state, that it is their mission to restore the Constitution with its proper balance among the three branches of the federal government. We must save self-government from the rule of judges. The whole future of America depends on it.

Judges Censor
Acknowledgment of God

FOR DECADES, the Pledge of Allegiance has been re-cited daily by millions of schoolchildren. Depictions of the Ten Commandments appear on thousands of public properties, including the U.S. Supreme Court. Against the wishes of Congress, state legislatures, and the American people, unelected judges have been assaulting our right to acknowledge God.

Lawsuits filed by atheists may soon target other acknowledgments of God. Our national motto is "In God We Trust," and it is enshrined on our currency. In our National Anthem, we sing "In God is our trust" and "Praise the Power that hath made and preserved us a Nation."

All three branches of the federal government, as well as our military, have always acknowledged God. Congress opens each session with a prayer. The President issues Thanksgiving and other proclamations acknowledging God and usually ends his speeches with "God bless America."

The U.S. Supreme Court starts each day with "God save the United States and this Honorable Court." All public officials, including the President and all judges, swear an oath to uphold the Constitution "so help me God." Most of us use this same oath when we swear to tell the truth in legal proceedings. These customs have persisted for more than two centuries.

Our nation's founding document, the Declaration of Independence, acknowledges God as our Creator, Supreme Lawgiver, Supreme Judge, Source of all Rights, and Patron and Protector.

God has been specifically acknowledged in all state constitutions. Among the powers reserved to the states under the Tenth Amendment of the U.S. Constitution is surely the power to write their own constitutions.

Nothing in the Constitution confers on the federal courts the final authority to decide how other entities of government may acknowledge God.

ASSAULT ON THE PLEDGE

Despite the tremendous role that the Pledge of Allegiance has played in American life for many decades, on June 26, 2002, the Ninth Circuit U.S. Court of Appeals handed down a 2 to 1 ruling in *Newdow v. U.S. Congress* banning the Pledge of Allegiance from the public schools because of its words "under God." The dissenting judge emphasized how ridiculous it is to claim that the Pledge of Allegiance violates the Establishment Clause of the First Amendment: "Such phrases as 'In God We Trust' and 'under God' have no tendency to establish a religion in this country or to suppress anyone's exercise, or non-exercise, of religion, except in the fevered eye of persons who most fervently would like to drive all tincture of religion out of the public life of our polity. Those expressions have not caused any real harm of that sort over the years since 1791, and are not likely to do so in the future."

When the Ninth Circuit on March 4, 2003, voted to deny the request for a rehearing *en banc*, one of the dissenting judges asked, "Does atheism become the default religion protected by the Establishment Clause?"

Congress's reaction to the *Newdow* decision was dramatic. On the same day as the original anti-Pledge ruling, a resolution of appropriate indignation was adopted by the U.S. House of Representatives by a vote of 416 to 3 and by a Senate vote of 99 to 1. When the full Ninth Circuit refused to reconsider this outrageous decision, the House reaffirmed its support for the Pledge by a vote of 400 to 7, and the Senate did likewise by 94 to 0.

Two cheers for Congress. But words are cheap, and Congress has done nothing substantial to fulfill its constitutional duty to correct this judicial outrage.

When the *Newdow* case reached the Supreme Court in the summer of 2004, the justices decided to duck the issue and dismissed it on the technicality that Newdow lacked standing to sue. As Chief Justice Rehnquist said in his dissent, this technicality was "like the proverbial excursion ticket—good for this day only."

This evasion saved the Court the embarrassment of confronting the argument that the abolition of "under God" in the Pledge would be the logical result of its long series of anti-religion decisions. As Justice Thomas wrote in his concurrence, "adherence to *Lee* would require us to strike down the Pledge policy." *Lee v. Weisman* (1992) was the decision banning school invocations, which is now gleefully cited in all anti-God litigation.

Before we rejoice that public school children may continue to recite the Pledge, we should face the fact that five of the nine justices (including Justice Kennedy) voted to dismiss the *Newdow* case on procedural grounds alone. They were eager to outlaw the Pledge, but probably feared that such a decision might help to re-elect George W. Bush in November. The justices decided to wait for a more opportune time. Newdow brought another case and on September 14, 2005 successfully got a Jimmy Carter–appointed judge in California to rule the Pledge in public schools unconstitutional again.

Newdow's case was not the only one of its kind. In July 2003, a federal judge barred Pennsylvania teachers from obeying a state law requiring them to lead their classes in reciting the Pledge or singing the National Anthem. On appeal, the Third Circuit unanimously affirmed this decision (*Circle School v. Pappert*, 2004). In August 2003, the ACLU persuaded another federal district judge to block a Colorado law requiring teachers to lead the Pledge, even though the law had a religious exception and exempted teachers who were not U.S. citizens.

Public opinion has always been strongly in favor of having schoolteachers lead the Pledge. Children are not compelled to join in the recitation if it is contrary to their religion, but one atheist parent should not be permitted to silence the entire class. Massachusetts Governor Michael Dukakis's veto of a state law requiring teachers to lead the Pledge became a major issue in the 1988 Presidential campaign and helped to elect George H.W. Bush.

ONE NATION UNDER GOD

The First Amendment states: "Congress shall make no law respecting an establishment of religion, or prohibiting the free exercise thereof; . . ." The American Civil Liberties Union (ACLU), atheist lawyers, and activist judges have been trying to make us believe that the acknowledgment of God by public officials, or by anyone on public property, is a violation of those words and therefore must cease. They are acting contrary to what the First Amendment says as well as to our entire political and legal tradition.

God has always been part of the American ideology and experience. In the Declaration of Independence, Thomas Jefferson described our rights as God-given. This means that our rights are natural and inborn, not a grant from a king or the government.

The term "nation under God" as used in the Pledge of Allegiance was popularized by President Abraham Lincoln in the Gettysburg Address in 1863: ". . . a new nation, conceived in liberty and dedicated to the proposition that all men are created equal . . . that this nation under God shall have a new birth of freedom, and that government of the people, by the people, for the people, shall not perish from the earth." It is ludicrous to suggest that Thomas Jefferson or Abraham Lincoln was trying to establish a religion.

In the 1950s, during the Cold War, the phrase "nation under God" gained increased popularity as a way of distinguishing America from "godless communism," which was aggressively atheistic and intolerant of religion. Our leaders preferred to describe America in positive, not negative, terms. They didn't want to say "we have individual rights because we're not ruled by kings or commies." Jefferson and Lincoln were known for their eloquence, and saying we are a "nation under God" is surely a better way of endorsing our traditional American ideals.

Atheist pressure groups and activist judges are now claiming that public acknowledgments of God are somehow unconstitutional. It's hard, though, to find Americans sincerely offended by the acknowledgment of God.

NEWDOW'S DAY IN COURT

When Dr. Michael Newdow personally appeared in oral argument to ask the Supreme Court to ban teachers from reciting "under God" in the Pledge of Allegiance, the atheists thought he had a compelling legal case. Over the last several decades, the Supreme Court again and again has censored and excluded prayer and morality from public life and schools.

A simple acknowledgment of God in public schools? A moment of silence in school? Posting the Ten Commandments in classrooms? A student-arranged invocation at graduation? A student-led prayer before a football game? The Supreme Court has said no, no, no, no, and no. In no other area of the law have the liberals enjoyed such a run-up of victories over such a long period of time.

The religion-haters' mischievous use of the federal courts has persisted because the American public has not been paying attention and because the legal community has propagated the myth that the Constitution is whatever the Supreme Court says it is.

Newdow looked at the long series of pro-atheist Supreme Court rulings and concluded that these precedents require removing "under God" from the Pledge. The atheists assumed the Court was ripe for the ultimate censorship to prevent our society from acknowledging the very nature of our existence. Their victory would relegate the Declaration of Independence, the Gettysburg Address, and countless presidential proclamations to the status of historical curiosities.

At the oral argument before the Supreme Court, Justice John Paul Stevens showed his hostility to religion by supporting Newdow. Justice David Souter expressed the secularists' argument that "under God" doesn't really mean under God, calling the Pledge's mention of God "so tepid, so diluted then so far, let's say, from a compulsory prayer that in fact it—it should be, in effect, beneath the constitutional radar." His metaphor was revealing; under the radar is exactly where the secularists want to conceal God, so that no reference to God is ever noticeable in public or in school.

Newdow probably thought he was scoring points in his oral argument when he said that adding the words "under God" to the Pledge in the 1950s was contrary to the spirit of its original purpose and divided the country between those who are religious and those who are not. Under questioning, he had to admit that "under God" was voted into the Pledge by an act of Congress that was "apparently unanimous." Chief Justice William Rehnquist commented, "Well, that doesn't sound divisive." Newdow retorted, "That's only because no atheist can get elected to public office." At that point, spectators broke into spontaneous applause, confirming that most Americans do not want atheists running our country.

The day after the oral argument, an Associated Press poll reported that nine out of ten Americans want "under God" to remain in the Pledge. When President Bush was asked during his second presidential debate in 2004 what kind of judge he would nominate to the Supreme Court, he replied, "I wouldn't pick a judge who said that the Pledge of Allegiance couldn't be said in a school because it had the words 'under God' in it."

THE TEN COMMANDMENTS ON TRIAL

The Supreme Court banned the Ten Commandments from public school classrooms in 1980. Private funds had been raised to place framed depictions of the Ten Commandments in Kentucky classrooms, but in *Stone v. Graham* the Supreme Court ordered them removed.

That action by the judicial supremacists started a national campaign to remove the Ten Commandments from public buildings and parks all over the country. Most of these lawsuits were instigated by the American Civil Liberties Union or Americans United for Separation of Church and State.

Since 1980, twenty-eight cases have been filed to challenge displays of the Ten Commandments in public buildings, squares and parks, including twenty-four since 1999. In Utah the ACLU even announced a scavenger hunt with a prize for anyone who could find another Ten Commandments monument that the ACLU could persuade an activist judge to remove. These monuments are worth a lot of money to the ACLU because federal law allows generous legal fees to be recovered for every Ten Commandments lawsuit the ACLU wins.

The most famous Ten Commandments case unfolded in Montgomery, Alabama, where the ACLU sued to force removal of a Ten Commandments monument that had been installed in the colonnaded rotunda of the Alabama State Judicial Building on August 1, 2001, by Alabama Chief Justice Roy Moore. Shaped like a cube, this four-foot-tall monument displayed the Ten Commandments on the top. Each of the four sides of the cube featured famous American words: "Laws of nature and of nature's God" from the Declaration of Independence (1776), "In God We Trust" from our national motto (1956), "One nation under God, indivisible, with liberty and justice for all" from our Pledge of Allegiance (1954), and "So help me God" from the oath of office in the Judiciary Act (1789). The remaining space on the sides of the cube was filled with quotations from famous Americans such as George Washington, Thomas Jefferson and our first Chief Justice John Jay, from British jurist William Blackstone, and from our National Anthem.

The ACLU filed suit to have the monument removed, and found a Carter-appointed federal judge willing to intervene in a state court matter. Myron H. Thompson was confirmed as a federal judge by the Democrat-controlled Senate in 1980 just a few months before the Reagan landslide.

Judge Thompson held a week-long trial, then ruled the Ten Commandments monument unconstitutional and ordered it removed from the State Judicial Building. It took him seventy-six pages to present his rationale in *Glassroth v. Moore* (2003). Thompson's principal holding was that "the Chief Justice's actions and intentions" violate the Establishment Clause of the First Amendment. Unable to demonstrate that the monument itself violates the First Amendment, Thompson rested his decision on Chief Justice Moore's speeches, writings, campaign literature, and associations.

Thompson, who personally went to view the monument, pronounced "the solemn ambience of the rotunda" and "sacred aura" about the monument as additional reasons why it is unconstitutional. He pretended to see the "sloping top" of the Ten Commandments tablets as unconstitutionally making the viewer think that they are an open Bible in disguise.

The "aura" about the monument was augmented, he said, by its location "in front of a large picture window with a waterfall in the background," so that you really can't miss seeing the monument. Thompson concluded that "a reasonable observer" would "feel as though the State of Alabama is advancing or endorsing, favoring or preferring, Christianity." It surely is a non sequitur to say that a picture window and waterfall somehow transform the Ten Commandments, which belong to Jewish law, into an endorsement of Christianity.

Judge Thompson ordered the Ten Commandments removed because three attorney plaintiffs "consider the monument offensive. It makes them feel like outsiders." But no atheist has any plausible claim to be offended by a reference to something he thinks does not exist. Atheists feign offense simply as a way to censor expressions of faith by others. In any case, nobody has a constitutional right not to be offended.

The strangest lines in this opinion were Judge Thompson's repeated references to Chief Justice Moore's belief in "the Judeo-Christian God." Thompson accused Moore of "an obvious effort to proselytize" on behalf of his Judeo-Christian religion and even of being "uncomfortably too close" to supporting the adoption of a "theocracy." Thompson said it would be "unwise and even dangerous" to define the word "religion" in the First Amendment, but then used the word "religion" or "religious" 149 times in his opinion.

This case had nothing to do with establishing a religion or a church, which the Establishment Clause forbids. The case simply posed the question whether the First Amendment prohibits us from acknowledging God on public property or in a public forum, and the answer should be no.

JUDICIAL CAT-AND-MOUSE

In Duluth, Minnesota, a controversy over a Ten Commandments monument donated by the Fraternal Order of Eagles, which stood outside its city hall for forty-seven years, led to thirteen months of wrangling, public rallies, a lawsuit, and 140 published letters to the editor. The *Duluth News Tribune* urged settlement out of fear that paying the ACLU's attorney's fees could cost the city up to $90,000. In October 2004, to settle the lawsuit, the city council moved the monument to property owned by Comfort Suites.

Hoping to avoid litigation, LaCrosse, Wisconsin, sold its Ten Commandments monument and the land under it to the Fraternal Order of Eagles, which had donated it to the city years earlier. The Freedom from Religion Foundation sued the city anyway. A Carter-appointed federal judge ordered the city to "undo the sale" and remove the monument. The Seventh Circuit reversed that decision in 2005.

In a Missouri town named Humansville, population 950, the school district is paying $45,000 to a woman who sued to get an activist judge to order the removal of a Ten Commandments plaque the size of a legal pad that had been hanging on the cafeteria wall for six years.

In Nebraska, an anonymous ACLU atheist sued the city of Plattsmouth to remove a Ten Commandments monument (that he claims "alienates" him) which is situated in an isolated corner of a large city park. He won his case before an Eighth Circuit panel, but the full Eighth Circuit overturned that decision in August 2005.

Everett, Washington, spent $70,000 defending a granite Ten Commandments monument that stood for decades in front of its old city hall.

The Sixth Circuit in *ACLU of Ohio v. Ashbrook* (2004) upheld a district court ruling that a state court judge must remove a Ten Commandments poster from his courtroom. He also displayed a Bill of Rights poster, but that didn't save him.

Five Georgia counties placed Ten Commandments displays in their courthouses. A federal judge ordered one removed; the others face challenges.

A district court judge in the Tenth Circuit tossed out a suit challenging a Ten Commandments monument in Pleasant Grove Park in Salt Lake City, Utah, which had been donated by the Fraternal Order of Eagles in 1971.

By 2005, three federal circuits had held Ten Commandments displays unconstitutional, but four federal circuits and one state supreme court had held that the Ten Commandments are constitutional.

Finally, the U.S. Supreme Court dealt with the Ten Commandments issue in two inconsistent 5 to 4 decisions on June 27, 2005. In *Van Orden v. Perry*, the Court allowed the Ten Commandments to be displayed on the grounds of the Texas State Capitol, but in *McCreary County v. ACLU of Kentucky* the Court banished the Ten Commandments from courthouses.

According to the Court, displaying the Ten Commandments outside a building is permissible, but inside a building it is not. Since most of the hundreds of Ten Commandments monuments in the open air were installed as a promotion for Cecil B. DeMille's wonderful movie *The Ten Commandments*, that's acceptable because it had a secular motive. But the Ten Commandments display in the Kentucky courthouse was suspected of being installed with a religious motive, so the Supreme Court won't allow it.

The incoherence of these two decisions is evident in the Court's explanation of why the Ten Commandments must be removed from courthouses all over the country, but not from the walls of the Supreme Court building itself. The tablets that Moses is carrying, the Court argued, do not have all the words spelled out.

Justice Souter declared that "suing a state over religion puts nothing in a plaintiff's pocket." On the contrary, the lawsuits against religion that now clutter our courts are fueled by a federal law allowing enormous attorney's fees to the winners. When groups such as the ACLU win their cases, they receive extravagant attorney's fees at the expense of local taxpayers.

Barry Lynn, director of Americans United for Separation of Church and State, summed up the Supreme Court's long-awaited ruling: "These decisions guarantee there will be far more lawsuits." He is correct about that; decisions about the Ten Commandments on a case by case basis assure that we will have many more supremacist decisions based on the current whims of the justices.

PRAYER IN SCHOOLS

The judicial supremacists' war on the acknowledgment of God began in 1962 when the Supreme Court banned prayer in public schools in *Engel v. Vitale*. The prayer at issue in that case was in no way an establishment of religion or even a sectarian prayer. It simply read: "Almighty God, we acknowledge our dependence upon Thee, and we beg Thy blessing upon us, our parents, our teachers and our Country."

No school was ordered to use this prayer; it was merely recommended as a prayer that schools could use. No child was compelled to recite the prayer; children who did not wish to say the prayer could remain silent or leave the room. Teachers were forbidden to make any comment about a child who left the room.

Justice Potter Stewart's dissent went to the core of the problem: "The Court has misapplied a great constitutional principle. I cannot see how an 'official religion' is established by letting those who want to say a prayer say it. On the contrary, I think that to deny the wish of these school children to join in reciting this prayer is to deny them the opportunity of sharing in the spiritual heritage of our nation."

Engel v. Vitale is a major example of the new judicial supremacy embarked upon by what became known as the Warren Court, headed by Chief Justice Earl Warren from 1953 to 1969. *Engel* was widely criticized at the time. Legal scholars recognized that the Court was treading on new territory outside the proper scope of judicial authority.

In a major speech, Erwin Griswold, dean of the Harvard Law School, said the Court had no business voiding the prayer. "Congress had made no law," he said in reference to the wording of the First Amendment, and "those who wrote the 'establishment of religion' clause might be rather perplexed by the use which has been made of it in 1962."

Griswold said "it was unfortunate that the question involved in the *Engel* case was ever thought of as a matter for judicial decision." Furthermore, "it was unfortunate that the Court decided the case, one way or the other" because "there are some matters which are essentially local in nature . . . to be worked out by the people themselves in their own communities."

Pointing out that there was nothing compulsory about the prayer, Griswold added, "In a country which has a great tradition of tolerance, is it not important that minorities, who have benefited so greatly from that tolerance, should be tolerant, too?" But the minority atheists are supremely *in*tolerant, and they found judicial supremacists who were all too eager to overturn two centuries of American school-children's acknowledgment of God.

It's easy to track increased public dissatisfaction with the public schools from that date forward. In case after case since *Engel v. Vitale*, the Supreme Court has carried on a relentless campaign against any mention of God in public schools. The Supreme Court prohibited Kentucky from posting the Ten Commandments in schoolrooms (*Stone v. Graham*, 1980), and prohibited Alabama public schools from having a daily moment of silence "for prayer and meditation" (*Wallace v. Jaffree*, 1985).

When the Court banned a prayer at graduation ceremonies in *Lee v. Weisman* (1992), Justice Scalia said in his dissent that this decision "lays waste a tradition that is as old as public school graduation ceremonies themselves." By the year 2000, the Court had even banned prayers before football games (*Santa Fe Independent School District v. Doe*).

In 2003, the federal courts started to extend prayer bans to adults. The Fourth Circuit U.S. Court of Appeals declared that it is unconstitutional for cadets attending Virginia Military Institute, a strict state military college, to be required to remain silent while a student chaplain recites this invocation before supper: "Now O God, we receive this food and share this meal together with thanksgiving. Amen." Both the Fourth Circuit and the Supreme Court seemed to acknowledge that the plaintiffs had no standing to sue, but nevertheless allowed a ruling to stand that makes school officials personally financially liable if they reinstate the supper prayer (*Mellen v. Bunting*).

Another nationally prominent military college, the Citadel, then announced that it, too, would ban prayers rather than risk the expense of defending against a lawsuit. Prayers at other military academies are the ACLU's next targets.

Chief Justice Rehnquist stated in *Santa Fe Independent School District v. Doe* that the Court "bristles with hostility to all things religious in public life." Judge Bork says that activist judges are so thoroughly secularized that "they not only reject personal belief but maintain an active hostility to religion and religious institutions." The Supreme Court "has almost succeeded in establishing a new religion: secular humanism." Under recent First Amendment decisions, nude dancing before school football games would be a more acceptable form of expression than prayer.

CROSSES AND SEALS

The atheists have carried on a fifteen-year battle to get supremacist judges to remove a twenty-nine-foot cross first erected some seventy years ago atop Mount Soledad in La Jolla, California, as a memorial to World War I veterans. There had never been a complaint until the ACLU filed suit, calling the cross a violation of the Establishment Clause. The ACLU has so far collected $63,000 in attorney's fees for legal victories along the way. As part of the public campaign to save the cross, Congress passed a law, signed by President Bush, declaring it a national war memorial.

But on October 7, 2005, a state court judge ruled it unconstitutional to transfer the cross and the land under it to the federal government under the deal approved by 76 percent of the voters in a special election on July 26. The judge called the transfer "an unconstitutional preference of the Christian religion to the exclusion of other religions and non-religious beliefs."

The atheists have carried on similar campaigns to remove depictions of a cross in any county or city seal. Many local government entities surrender rather than risk the costs to defend the seal, especially when costs include not only their own attorney's fees, but the ACLU's as well.

The ACLU demanded that Los Angeles County remove a tiny cross from the Los Angeles County seal, one of nearly a dozen symbols included in the seal. One look at the seal shows how ridiculous this demand was. A third of the seal and the centerpiece is the Greek goddess Pomona standing on the shore of the Pacific Ocean. The ACLU doesn't object to her; portrayals of pagan goddesses are acceptable. Both side sections of the seal depict California motifs: the Spanish galleon *San Salvador*, a tuna fish, a cow, the Hollywood Bowl, two stars representing the movie and television industries, oil derricks, and a couple of engineering instruments that signify Los Angeles' industrial construction and space exploration. The cross is so tiny that it doesn't even have its own section and consumes perhaps two percent of the seal's space.

Removing the cross is a blatant attempt to erase history, to drop it down the Memory Hole, as George Orwell would say. It is just as reasonable to recognize the historical fact that California was settled by Christians who built missions all over the state as it is to honor the Spanish ship, the *San Salvador*, which sailed into San Pedro Harbor (named after St. Peter) on October 8, 1542. Nevertheless, the county caved in to the ACLU's threats and began to spend $700,000 to put a newly designed seal on buildings, cars, employee uniforms, letterheads, and websites.

The atheists and secularists who are determined to wipe out any public recognition of religion are indefatigable in seeking plaintiffs for their litigation. In addition to the many Christmastime challenges to Nativity scenes, targets in the last couple of years have included:

- An open Bible under glass inside a four-foot stone monument near the entrance to a courthouse in Houston that was erected as a memorial to philanthropist William S. Mosher. (The judge in *Staley v. Harris County* ordered the county to remove the

Bible "within ten days" and to pay plaintiff "$40,586 in attorney's fees and expenses within ten days.") The case is on appeal to the Fifth Circuit.

- A Theodore Roosevelt quotation engraved on the mahogany walls of one of Riverside, California's oldest courtrooms that reads "The true Christian is the true citizen."

- "In God We Trust" on the front of the Davidson County (North Carolina) Government Center.

- Christmas trees in public buildings in Pasco County, Florida, which allegedly were religious symbols.

THE ACLU'S WAR ON THE BOY SCOUTS

The American Civil Liberties Union has sued the Boy Scouts fourteen times over the last twenty-five years. The ACLU objects to the Boy Scout oath: "On my honor, I will do my best to do my duty to God and my country, and to obey the Scout Law, to help other people at all times, to keep myself physically strong, mentally awake and morally straight." Those policies have been building character in boys for the last ninety years. Character development and value-based leadership training are central to the Boy Scouts' mission. Most Americans think the Boy Scouts is a terrific organization that trains boys to be better citizens.

In the most widely publicized of these court cases, *Boy Scouts v. Dale* (2000), the Supreme Court ruled 5 to 4 to uphold the right of the Boy Scouts to prevent homosexuals from being Scout leaders. Despite losing that case, the ACLU has continued to harass the Boy Scouts and try to chase them off all public properties. The ACLU claims the Boy Scout oath violates the First Amendment if recited on public property.

In December 2004, the U.S. Department of Defense caved in to an ACLU lawsuit and agreed to stop sponsoring four hundred Boy Scout troops and to warn military bases worldwide not to directly sponsor Boy Scout troops.

For over two decades, the Boy Scouts have held a quadrennial jamboree on military property in Virginia attracting forty thousand Scouts and three hundred thousand parents and spectators. The federal Jamboree Statute authorized the Secretary of Defense to loan equipment necessary for the event. In July 2005, federal district court Judge Blanche M. Manning, a Clinton appointee, knocked out the Jamboree law in *Winkler v. Chicago School Reform Board of Trustees*. She didn't bother to hold a trial on the issue; she just enjoined the government from obeying the Jamboree statute.

The ACLU is now carrying on a campaign to get supremacist judges to expel the Boy Scouts from every public school in the country. In 2005 the ACLU threatened the Boy Scouts with massive litigation if they did not abandon all their school charters. The Scouts have been trying to find non-school sponsors so they can meet at public schools as an independent group.

OUR RELIGIOUS HERITAGE

The banning of the acknowledgment of God from public life and from public schools is not required by the Constitution. It is a malicious campaign invented and pursued by the judicial supremacists of the last fifty years. Previously, the Court's attitude toward religion was eloquently stated in the 1892 Supreme Court decision of *Church of the Holy Trinity v. United States*: "No purpose of action against religion can be imputed to any legislation, state or national, because this is a religious people. This is historically true. From the discovery of this continent to the present hour, there is a single voice making this affirmation."

The Court listed the religious origins of our society such as the first colonial grant to Sir Walter Raleigh in 1584, the first charter of Virginia in 1606, the Fundamental Orders of Connecticut in 1638-39, the charter of privileges granted by William Penn to Pennsylvania in 1701, the Declaration of Independence, and the constitutions of all the individual states. Concluding, the Supreme Court ruled: "There is no dissonance in these declarations. There is a universal language pervading them all, having one meaning; they affirm and reaffirm that this is a religious nation. These are not individual sayings, declarations of private persons: they are organic utterances; they speak the voice of the entire people."

As late as 1952, none other than Supreme Court Justice William O. Douglas wrote that "We are a religious people whose institutions presuppose a Supreme Being" (*Zorach v. Clauson*). But since 1962, the judicial supremacists have been fiercely determined to expurgate every mention of religion from the schoolhouse.

Justice Scalia's dissent in the 2005 case that held the Ten Commandments in the Kentucky courthouse unconstitutional (*McCreary County v. ACLU of Kentucky*) is an eloquent and current recitation of America's religious heritage, showing why it is simply not true, as the Court's majority proclaimed, that "the First Amendment mandates governmental neutrality between . . . religion and nonreligion."

The issue of the acknowledgment of God will not go away. The notorious *Lemon* test, first announced in *Lemon v. Kurtzman* (1971), encourages the filing of lawsuits so that activist judges can censor any mention of God or religion on the ground that it has a religious purpose, has a religious effect, or increases an entanglement of government with religion. This permits judicial supremacists to manipulate the test any way that suits them.

What damage will the Supreme Court do with its next dozen cases on religion? Will the American people allow the judicial supremacists to continue denying our heritage, keeping our children ignorant of our history, changing our culture, and censoring our precious words? Or, are we going to put a stop to the usurpations of the activist judges? That is our challenge.

− 3 −

Judges Redefine Marriage

THE DEFINITION OF MARRIAGE as the union of a man and woman as husband and wife has prevailed throughout our legal history. Gay activists have been eager for years to get the government to issue marriage licenses to same-sex couples. Unable to persuade the American people, the gay lobby has sought out activist judges to assert judicial supremacy.

The gays achieved their first victory in Hawaii. In 1993, the Hawaii state supreme court ruled that the denial of marriage licenses to same sex couples was discriminatory and unconstitutional under Hawaii's state Equal Rights Amendment, which mandates "equality . . . on account of sex." The people of Hawaii then rebuked the court, passing a constitutional amendment in 1998 to overturn the *Baehr v. Lewin* decision. A similar decision was rendered by a lower court in Alaska in 1998, and that decision was overturned by a state constitutional amendment that same year.

The next move was in Vermont in 1999, where the state supreme court ordered the state legislature to grant all the benefits and privileges of marriage to same-sex couples. The Vermont state legislature should not have allowed the court to tell it what statute to pass, but it did, and in 2000 Vermont governor Howard Dean signed the nation's first "civil union" law.

On November 18, 2003, Massachusetts judges shocked the nation. It's hard to find a more outrageous example of activist judges asserting judicial supremacy than the 4 to 3 decision in *Goodridge v. Department of Public Health* by the Massachusetts supreme court mandating same-sex marriage licenses. The Massachusetts state constitution was written by John Adams and adopted in 1780, and any notion that it was intended to include same-sex marriage is absurd. With elitist arrogance, the slim four-person majority bragged: "Certainly our decision today marks a significant change in the definition of marriage as it has been inherited from the common law, and understood by many societies for centuries."

Indeed, it does. The Massachusetts court even issued a special advisory opinion telling the legislature what sort of marriage law to pass (*Opinions of the Justices to the Senate,* February 3, 2004).

After acknowledging that for three centuries Massachusetts defined civil marriage as stated in Black's Law Dictionary—"the legal union of a man and woman as husband and wife"—the Massachusetts judicial supremacists declared that there is no "rational basis" for that definition, and ordered this new definition of marriage: "We construe civil marriage to mean the voluntary union of two persons as spouses, to the exclusion of all others."

Contrary to the Massachusetts decision, there is indeed a "rational basis" for the unanimity of the state and federal legislatures throughout American history that marriage should be publicly recognized as the union of a husband and a wife. The American people and our elected representatives have concluded that marriage is a moral good to be protected and encouraged. All social science statistics confirm that traditional marriage is good for women, good for men, good for children, and good for society.

Massachusetts judges had no authority to change the definition of marriage. They simply convinced themselves that they alone could change social policy and make new law. They did no analysis of the consequences of the social policy they mandated.

The dissenting judges in the Massachusetts same-sex marriage case understood that judicial supremacy was the underlying offense in this shocking decision: "What is at stake in this case is not the unequal treatment of individuals or whether individual rights have been impermissibly burdened, but the power of the Legislature to effectuate social change without interference from the courts.... The power to regulate marriage lies with the Legislature, not with the judiciary."

A concurring opinion in *Goodridge v. Department of Public Health* cited the Massachusetts state Equal Rights Amendment as one authority for the decision to legalize same-sex marriages. The state ERA was added as Article CVI of the Massachusetts Constitution in 1976. It provides that

"Equality under the law shall not be denied or abridged because of sex, race, color, creed or national origin."

Judge Cordy's dissent (joined by both other dissenting judges) reminded the court that just before the 1976 election when the voters adopted the state ERA, the official Massachusetts commission charged with the duty of advising the voters about ERA's effect issued this statement: "An equal rights amendment will have no effect upon the allowance or denial of homosexual marriages. The equal rights amendment is not concerned with the relationship of two persons of the same sex; it only addresses those laws or public-related actions which treat persons of opposite sexes differently."

The *Goodridge* decision's partial reliance on the Massachusetts ERA to legalize marriage between people of the same sex caused UCLA law professor Eugene Volokh to post on his website: "Phyllis Schlafly said it would be like this." Volokh concluded: "So the Massachusetts ERA did contribute to constitutional protection for homosexual marriage—as the opponents of the ERA predicted, and as the supporters of the ERA vehemently denied."

It is fortunate that the proposed *federal* Equal Rights Amendment was defeated in a ten-year legislative battle, from 1972 to 1982. The word used in the Amendment was "sex" (not women, as many were falsely led to believe), so the ERA if ratified would have given the mantle of the U.S. Constitution to same-sex marriages.

The Massachusetts case is part of a national gay rights strategy to make same-sex marriage a new constitutional right. The legal advocacy firm called Freedom to Marry is joined in this effort by the Gay & Lesbian Advocates & Defenders (GLAD), the ACLU, Lambda Legal, NOW Legal Defense and Education Fund, and Human Rights Watch. They seek from judicial supremacists what they cannot win from elected legislatures.

It is unfortunate that Massachusetts' public officials responded to the assault on marriage with words but not actions. Protesting that they oppose same-sex marriage, they knuckled under to the judicial supremacists and echoed the mantra that the court's decision is the law of the land. The failure of Massachusetts' elected officials promptly to use every legal weapon at their disposal to protect marriage encouraged judicial activists in other states, notably California, to indulge in similar same-sex mischief.

TAKING SIDES IN THE CULTURE WAR

The gay activists' campaign to bypass the legislative process and use judicial supremacists to achieve their goals has been going on for some years. In *Romer v. Evans* (1996), the Supreme Court overturned the decision of the majority of the people of Colorado who, by statewide referendum, had prohibited localities from granting a special protected status to homosexuals. Without any authority from the Constitution or citation of any applicable legal precedent, the Court ruled that Colorado's Amendment 2 was without a rational basis and was "born of animosity" toward homosexuals.

It would be more accurate to say that the Supreme Court's own decision was without a constitutional basis and was born of animosity toward traditional moral standards and people who hold them sacred. Animosity is apparently a quality that judicial supremacists, but not voters, are permitted to have.

In *Romer*, Justice Anthony Kennedy's majority decision stated: "Amendment 2 confounds this normal process of judicial review. It is at once too narrow and too broad." When Justice Kennedy said that Amendment 2 confounded judicial review, he meant that it confounded judicial supremacy. Amendment 2 would have limited the ability of the judges to invent new rights for homosexuals. When Kennedy said Amendment 2 was both "too narrow and too broad," he was spouting a contradiction to cover his failure to find any constitutional justification for invalidating Colorado's law.

In *Romer*, there was no case or controversy in the usual sense; there were some homosexuals and leftists who thought the amendment was bad policy, and the Court agreed. Amendment 2 was very simple and straightforward; the majority of Colorado voters understood its purpose and approved it. When Kennedy denied that Amendment 2 had "any identifiable legitimate purpose," he was taking sides in the culture war.

The same-sex-marriage activists know that the legal profession is predisposed to redefine marriage. The dissenting justices in *Lawrence v. Texas* (the 2003 Supreme Court decision that voided the Texas sodomy law) warned that the Supreme Court is imbued with the "law profession's anti-anti-homosexual culture." As Justice Scalia said in his dissent, *Lawrence v. Texas* "is the product of a law-profession culture, that has largely signed on to the so-called homosexual agenda," and "the Court has taken sides in the culture war." The *Goodridge* decision mandating same-sex marriage licenses was the predictable consequence of *Lawrence v. Texas.*

The out-of-the-mainstream attitudes expressed in the majority opinion in *Lawrence v. Texas* dealt a devastating blow to long-standing American laws and beliefs about morals and self-government, striking down our right to legislate against immoral actions, and doing so without advancing any argument that reasonably relates to the U.S. Constitution. No constitutional argument justified the decision that created the new right of sodomy. The decision evolved out of the social preferences of the justices and their pandering to liberal elites.

Justice Kennedy, who wrote the majority opinion, based it on "an emerging awareness that liberty gives substantial protection to adult persons in deciding how to conduct their private lives." It's obvious that using the criterion of "emerging awareness" gives much more latitude to the judicial supremacists who want to impose their avant-garde doctrines than does adhering to the Constitution, the text of the laws, and the intent of the people.

In *Lawrence v. Texas*, Justice Kennedy overturned a U.S. Supreme Court precedent of only seventeen years earlier (*Bowers v. Hardwick*, 1986). This is the same Justice Kennedy who upheld legalized abortion in *Planned Parenthood v. Casey* (1992) on the ground that the Court's legitimacy depends on upholding the *Roe v. Wade* ruling of nineteen years earlier. This is also the same Justice Kennedy who thumbed his nose at the votes of the majority of Coloradans in *Romer v. Evans* in 1996.

NOT A CIVIL RIGHTS ISSUE

Whining about discrimination, the gay lobby is trying to position the Massachusetts ruling as a logical expansion of the 1960s civil rights movement. It isn't. Gays can already get marriage licenses on exactly the same terms as anyone else. Everyone is equally barred from marrying another person who is under a certain age, or too closely related, or of the same sex, or already married to another. Sound reasons underlie all these requirements, which apply equally to everyone, male and female.

Same-sex marriage licenses are not needed to permit a small number of people to choose alternative lifestyles; they are already doing that. Gays already have the liberty to live their lives as they choose, create partnerships, set up housekeeping, share income and expenses, make contracts and wills, and transfer property.

What gays now demand is public approval and government support for a lifestyle that others believe is immoral (like adultery and bigamy). That amounts to the minority forcing the majority to license what it disapproves. It would force the rest of us to accept a public judgment that personal desire outweighs the value of traditional marriage and the need of children for a married mother and a father. It would give entitlements to gay couples in the areas of tax policy, education and classroom curricula, adoption, government spending, the military, and Social Security benefits.

Advocates of same-sex marriage pretend that the applicant gays are the only relevant parties. That is plainly false since any license is an authorization by the state for the benefit of the public. Legislatures, not courts, should have the power to decide whether to issue a new type of license for marriage.

If personal desire is to become the only criterion for public recognition of marriage, if equal rights and nondiscrimination require us to be neutral about who is eligible for marriage, how then can we deny marriage to those who want to marry a child, or a very close relative, or more than one wife? These practices are common in some countries.

If a thirteen-year-old girl can exercise "choice" to "control her own body" and get an abortion, why can't she have the choice to marry? The *Goodridge* decision ruled that "the right to marry means little if it does not include the right to marry the person of one's choice."

The equal protection and equal rights arguments of the homosexuals are totally phony and are clear admissions that the homosexuals intend to achieve their goals through the courts. America does not treat everyone equally, and the Constitution does not require it. The treatment of individuals under the federal income tax law is dramatically unequal. Many valid laws give benefits or protections to designated groups, such as widows (in the Social Security system), to children (in anti-pornography legislation), and to various people based on need. Many laws impose obligations unequally on designated groups (such as military draft registration and service). State governments grant and deny licenses for dozens of activities, from fishing to gun ownership, using regulations that discriminate among different groups. They are certainly constitutionally justified in licensing traditional marriage but not licensing disfavored marital arrangements.

Traditional marriage is based on the beautiful words "to have and to hold from this day forward, for better for worse, for richer for poorer, in sickness and in health, forsaking all others, to love and to cherish, till death do us part." Marriage must continue to be recognized as the essential unit of a stable society wherein husbands and wives provide a home and role models for the rearing of children. The American people and our elected representatives absolutely have a rational basis for concluding that marriage between a man and a woman should be protected and encouraged. Marriage must not be changed to mean merely two consenting persons agreeing to share quarters and apply to the government and employers for economic benefits.

When the famous French commentator Alexis de Toqueville traveled the United States in the mid-nineteenth century, he recognized that respect for marriage is very American: "There is certainly no country in the world where the tie of marriage is more respected than in America, or where conjugal happiness is more highly or worthily appreciated. . . . While the European endeavors to forget his domestic troubles by agitating society, the American derives from his own home that love of order which he afterwards carries with him into public affairs."

President George W. Bush, in his 2004 State of the Union Address, properly labeled "activist judges" as the enemy of traditional values and urged us to use "the constitutional process" to remedy the problem. Bush called on Americans to defend marriage against activist judges who force "their arbitrary will" by court order "without regard for the will of the people and their elected representatives."

THE BALLOT BOX VS. THE JUDGES

Citizens in many states responded to the challenge from supremacist judges by passing state constitutional amendments to define marriage as the union of one man and one woman. Nebraska passed such a state constitutional amendment in 2000, Nevada in 2002, thirteen other states did likewise in 2004, Kansas and Texas joined the list in 2005. Added to the Hawaii and Alaska amendments passed in 1998, that makes nineteen states that have passed constitutional amendments to protect traditional marriage. Several more states are expected to vote in 2006.

However, the judicial supremacists struck again in *Citizens for Equal Protection v. Bruning* (2005). U.S. District Judge Joseph Bataillon repudiated the 70 percent of Nebraskans who voted for this constitutional amendment. Here is its language: "Only marriage between a man and a woman shall be valid or recognized in Nebraska. The uniting of two persons of the same sex in a civil union, domestic partnership or other similar same-sex relationship shall not be valid or recognized in Nebraska." Appointed by President Clinton, Judge Bataillon's salient credential was his service as the Nebraska Democratic Party State Chairman from 1993-95.

His argument that the Nebraska law violates the First Amendment because it "chills or inhibits advocacy" of same-sex marriages is a legal embarrassment: gays can continue to advocate their agenda all they want. Bataillon's argument that the Nebraska law unfairly prohibits people from "entering into numerous relationships or living arrangements" is also far-fetched. Under the Nebraska law, gays can have any relationships they want, but they do not have the right to force the government or the people of Nebraska to recognize those relationships or accord them special privileges.

Same-sex marriage advocates have launched an attack on the federal Defense of Marriage Act (DOMA), which was overwhelmingly passed by Congress in 1996: 342 to 67 in the House, 85 to 14 in the Senate. It was signed by President Clinton, and Senator John Kerry was one of the few who voted against it.

DOMA does two things. First, in everything that is touched by federal law or regulation, "the word 'marriage' means only a legal union between one man and one woman as husband and wife," and "spouse refers only to a person of the opposite sex who is a husband or a wife." Second, Congress used its power under the "full faith and credit" provision of the Constitution to legislate that no state can be required to recognize another state's adoption of same-sex marriage.

In compliance with the federal DOMA, thirty-nine states have enacted their own state DOMAs, and nineteen states put defense of marriage in their state constitutions. Even liberal California passed a voter initiative (Proposition 22) in 2000 to protect marriage with 61 percent of the vote.

But the gay-rights lobby is determined to knock out DOMA. It survived the first two lawsuits against it, one in Florida and one in California, but lawyers and commentators predict that it's only a matter of time before a judge declares it unconstitutional.

Will Congress just grumble but do nothing to stop out-of-control judges from replacing self-government with their imperial edicts? If Congress fails to restrain judges from violating DOMA, we can expect anti-marriage atrocities to continue as an unelected judiciary remakes America into a society that undermines traditional marriage.

~ 4 ~

Judges Undermine
U.S. Sovereignty

EVERY FEDERAL OFFICIAL, including judges, upon taking office, takes this oath: "I, _____ , do solemnly swear (or affirm) . . . that I will support and defend the Constitution of the United States against all enemies, foreign and domestic; that I will bear true faith and allegiance to the same; . . . So help me God." What, therefore, should we say about a judge who bypasses the U.S. Constitution and laws and instead applies a foreign court's opinion? Is such a judge not faithless to his oath of office?

Yet such rulings have become more and more frequent. Six Supreme Court justices have cited foreign sources. Justice Stephen Breyer gleefully told George Stephanopoulos on ABC's *World News Tonight* how the United States is changing "through commerce and through globalization . . . [and] through immigration," and that this change is having an impact on the courts. He speculated on "the challenge" of whether our U.S. Constitution "fits into the governing documents of other nations."

Where did Justice Breyer get the idea that the U.S. Constitution should "fit" into the laws of other nations? If the United States can't make its own laws, we cannot be a sovereign nation. Justice Breyer admitted his dalliance with foreign opinions at a meeting of top-level French lawyers in Washington in November 2004 (where he delivered a third of his speech in French), and again at the American Bar Association Convention in Chicago on August 9, 2005.

In a dissent in *Knight v. Florida* (1999), Justice Breyer suggested that it was "useful" to consider court decisions on allowable delays of execution in India, Jamaica, and Zimbabwe. Zimbabwe, indeed, has had a lot of experience with executions, but it's hardly a country from which we should obtain guidance about due process.

Justice Kennedy couldn't find any language in the U.S. Constitution to justify overturning the Texas sodomy law in *Lawrence v. Texas* (2003), so he invoked "other authorities" to rationalize his "emerging awareness" that "liberty" now means that the judiciary can grant more license in matters of sex. These non-American authorities included a committee advising the British Parliament, decisions of the European Court of Human Rights, the European Convention on Human Rights, a brief filed by former United Nations High Commissioner for Human Rights Mary Robinson, and "other nations, too."

Kennedy overruled the Court's anti-sodomy decision, *Bowers v. Hardwick* (1986), brushing off what he called "the sweeping references by Chief Justice Burger [in that case] to the history of Western Civilization and to Judeo-Christian moral and ethical standards." The judicial supremacists think it is their mission to dictate a new regime of sexual mores to replace our Judeo-Christian moral and ethical standards, which they believe are obsolete.

Justice Kennedy wrote in *Lawrence v. Texas* that "The right the petitioners seek [to engage in homosexual sodomy] has been accepted as an integral part of human freedom in many other countries." Failing to mention the countries where sodomy is a serious crime, he emphasized the "values we share with a wider civilization." In fact, most other countries do not share American values, and we certainly don't want to share theirs.

Four other justices joined Kennedy's majority decision without distancing themselves from his globalist reasoning or his inaccurate recitation of the history of sodomy laws in this country. Justice Scalia eloquently dissented: "Constitutional entitlements do not spring into existence . . . because foreign nations decriminalize conduct." He called Kennedy's words "dangerous dicta," adding that the Supreme Court "should not impose foreign moods, fads or fashions on Americans."

Looking to foreign countries for guidance about U.S. laws or court decisions not only is an interference with our sovereignty, but will diminish the precious constitutional rights that Americans enjoy. The proposed Constitution for the European Union (EU) is completely different from our great, long-lasting United States Constitution. Our Bill of Rights sets forth a list of individual *rights* against the government, whereas the EU constitution includes a long list of *entitlements* to services to be provided by the government such as education, paid maternity leave, health care, housing, and environmental protection. The EU constitution purports to require "equality" between men and women, but sets up a program to give "specific advantages in favor of the underrepresented sex."

Instead of condemning Kennedy's use of foreign courts to change U.S. laws, the president of the American Bar Association opined that "the concept of fundamental law knows no national boundaries." Harvard law professor Laurence Tribe chimed in to "applaud" the "important insights" of the "global legal community."

This is deceptive. In fact, most other countries' "concept of fundamental law" is far removed from ours. Most other countries flatly reject precious American rights, spelled out in our Bill of Rights, such as trial by jury. Other countries' concepts of fundamental law may include such practices as same-sex marriages, polygamy, arranged marriages between cousins, so-called honor killings of women who reject the arrangements, cutting off hands as a punishment for theft, stoning to death as punishment for adultery, and prohibiting the private ownership of guns.

Justices Ruth Bader Ginsburg and Stephen Breyer, concurring in *Grutter v. Bollinger* (2003), cited a United Nations treaty to justify the University of Michigan Law School's racial preferences: "The International Convention on the Elimination of All Forms of Racial Discrimination, ratified by the United States in 1994 ... endorses special and concrete measures to ensure the adequate development and protection of certain racial groups ... for the purpose of guaranteeing them the full and equal enjoyment of human rights and fundamental freedoms."

The Senate ratified that treaty under pressure from the Clinton Administration thirty years after President Lyndon B. Johnson signed it. That is an example of how United Nations treaties come back to bite us by interfering with U.S. laws and customs.

In *Atkins v. Virginia* (2002), citing an amicus brief from the European Union, Justice John Paul Stevens rewrote the Eighth Amendment to outlaw capital punishment for those with low IQ scores. The EU warned us, Stevens wrote, that "within the world community, the imposition of the death penalty for crimes committed by mentally retarded offenders is overwhelmingly disapproved." Justice Scalia retorted, "The views of other nations cannot be imposed upon Americans." But five justices did impose foreign views on us.

Justices Stevens, Souter, and Ginsburg again turned to a foreign authority in writing a 2004 opinion. Dissenting from a decision in favor of private property rights, they invoked the views of a foreign supreme court justice for the purpose of departing from the plain meaning of U.S. laws (*BedRoc Limited v. United States*).

Although the U.S. Constitution specifically endorses capital punishment and puts no restrictions on age, Justice Anthony Kennedy's majority opinion in *Roper v. Simmons* (2005) cited foreign laws, "international opinion," and even an unratified treaty to rationalize overturning more than two hundred years of American law and history. Five justices—Kennedy, Ginsburg, Breyer, Stevens, and

Souter—rewrote the Eighth Amendment and overturned the laws of Alabama, Arizona, Arkansas, Delaware, Florida, Georgia, Idaho, Kentucky, Louisiana, Mississippi, Missouri, Nevada, New Hampshire, North Carolina, Oklahoma, Pennsylvania, South Carolina, Texas, Utah and Virginia, all states that allowed the death penalty for a seventeen-year-old who commits a particularly shocking murder. The murder involved in this case was extremely brutal and premeditated.

Kennedy's main argument was that he saw a "trend" against juvenile capital punishment in foreign countries: since 1989, seven countries (Iran, Pakistan, Saudi Arabia, Yemen, Nigeria, Congo, and China) have banned juvenile capital punishment. However, no such trend exists in the United States; since 1989, only four U.S. states have legislated against the juvenile death penalty (but none of them was executing juveniles anyway).

Kennedy claimed that most other countries don't execute seventeen-year-olds. But most other countries don't have due process–based capital punishment at all, so there is no distinction between criminals over and under age eighteen. Furthermore, most other countries don't allow jury trials or other guarantees found in the Bill of Rights, so who knows whether the accused ever gets what we would call a fair trial? More than 90 percent of jury trials are in the United States, and we certainly don't want to conform to non-jury-trial countries.

The five supremacist justices must think they can dictate the evolution of treaties as well as of the Constitution. They cited the United Nations Convention on the Rights of the Child, which our Senate year after year has refused to ratify. They also cited the International Covenant on Civil and Political Rights, which the Senate ratified only with a reservation specifically excluding the matter of juvenile capital punishment.

As Justice Scalia pointed out in dissent, the Court's invocation of foreign law is both contrived and disingenuous. The big majority of countries reject U.S.-style abortion on demand, but the supremacist justices conveniently ignore that international opinion. Justice Scalia summed it up like this: "the basic premise of the Court's argument—that American law should conform to the laws of the rest of the world—ought to be rejected out of hand."

Some state court judges are likewise infected with the itch to take guidance from foreign courts. The chief justice of the Massachusetts supreme judicial court (the court that issued the 2003 *Goodridge* decision demanding same-sex marriage licenses), Margaret Marshall, is "an advocate of mining the work of foreign courts," according to a writer for the journal *Legal Affairs*. That was the topic of Marshall's post-*Goodridge* lecture at New York University Law School. The reporter, who attended the lecture, received the clear impression that Marshall is strongly influenced by the high court of South Africa, which has promoted gay rights. Although Marshall (who is a South African native) did not cite a South African court in *Goodridge*, Harvard law professor Martha Minow, who has known Marshall for fifteen years, commented that *Goodridge* "is like a South Africa decision."

Justice Margaret Marshall did, however, cite the Canadian court that approved same-sex marriage. In one sentence, she managed to invoke foreign law, claim that judges can rewrite our country's laws, and slyly assert that the Constitution is evolving: "We concur with this [Canadian] remedy, which is entirely consonant with established principles of jurisprudence empowering a court to refine a common-law principle in light of evolving constitutional standards."

In March 2004, the European Court of Human Rights in Strasbourg ruled that laws preventing convicted prisoners from voting in elections are a breach of their human rights. The court ruled that it cannot accept "an absolute bar on voting by any serving prisoner . . . ."

Nearly all of America's fifty states deny the franchise to prisoners and also impose some kind of restriction on voting by convicted felons who have been released from prison. Will the Democrats now seek the votes of prisoners, citing the Strasbourg decision to persuade activist liberal judges to open up this new constituency?

THE GINSBURG-O'CONNOR TWO-STEP

Justices Ruth Bader Ginsburg and Sandra Day O'Connor apparently can't resist displaying their fascination with foreign opinion.

In August 2003, Ginsburg joined Hillary Clinton, Janet Reno, anti-Pledge-of-Allegiance judge Stephen Reinhardt, and other legal elites from Democratic administrations to launch a new organization called the American Constitution Society. Its mission is to challenge the Federalist Society, which supports constitutionalist judges and America's unique system of federalism.

A Jimmy Carter appointee, Judge Reinhardt, who may hold the modern record for being overturned the most times by the Supreme Court, set the tone of the conference, saying that the words "liberal judge" are not "dirty words." He urged judges to return to the liberal philosophy of Earl Warren, William Brennan, and William O. Douglas.

Ginsburg's contribution was to tell the American Constitution Society that "your perspective on constitutional law should encompass the world." She urged her colleagues to look beyond our borders in handling death penalty and homosexual rights cases. She added, "Our island or lone ranger mentality is beginning to change."

Justice O'Connor told the Southern Center for International Studies in Atlanta on October 31, 2003, that "I suspect that over time we will rely increasingly, or take notice at least increasingly, on international and foreign courts in examining domestic issues."

At a speech dedicating Georgetown University's new international law center on October 26, 2004, O'Connor said that international law "is vital if judges are to faithfully discharge their duties." She continued, "International law is a help in our search for a more peaceful world." She failed to give any example of international law preventing a war.

The effort to import international law into the United States has nothing to do with promoting peace. The purpose is to give a veneer of respectability to liberals who want to change our Constitution without obtaining approval of the American people through the amendment process.

Back on the public platform to address the American Society of International Law on April 1, 2005, Justice Ginsburg again endorsed the practice of consulting foreign and international law. She ridiculed the notion that "the U.S. Constitution is a document essentially frozen in time as of the date of its ratification"—forgetting that our Constitution has been successfully amended twenty-seven times since then.

INTERNATIONAL LAW IS POLITICS

In addition to the unacceptable citations of foreign laws, treaties, court opinions, and briefs to decide U.S. cases, we hear judges, lawyers, and politicians talking casually about "international law." That is not law as we understand the term at all; it is just international politics.

The people who seek global governance are using supremacist judges to put Americans in the noose of fabricated law (i.e., not passed by any legislature) written (usually ex post facto) by foreign bureaucrats or United Nations functionaries, and administered by foreign bureaucrats pretending to be judges. The goal of these globalists is the worldwide rule of judges.

A tremendous effort was made to lock the United States into the International Criminal Court (ICC) through a treaty negotiated during the Clinton Administration. Clinton signed the ICC treaty on New Year's Eve 2000, one of his last acts as president. Fortunately, President George W.

Bush *un*signed the ICC treaty in 2002. If the U.S. Senate had ratified the ICC, U.S. troops and even government officials would be subject to prosecution by a court in the Hague, where Americans would not, of course, have U.S. Bill of Rights protections such as trial by a jury of their peers.

The impudence of these foreign courts knows no bounds. The ICC claims jurisdiction over Americans even though we are not a party to the ICC treaty. Our government should never acquiesce in such judicial arrogance.

Further evidence of judicial power-grabbing includes the tribunals of the North American Free Trade Agreement (NAFTA). On February 6, 2001, a NAFTA tribunal ordered the United States to ignore U.S. environmental law and forthwith admit tens of thousands of Mexican trucks that do not meet U.S. standards. The NAFTA tribunal claimed to derive its authority from the NAFTA "treaty," but NAFTA was not (as it should have been) a treaty ratified by the Senate; it was an executive agreement implemented by an act of Congress passed by a simple majority vote. In *Department of Transporation v. Public Citizen* (2004), the Supreme Court voted 9 to 0 to allow the executive branch to implement the decision of the NAFTA tribunal ordering that U.S. roads be opened to Mexican trucks.

Another NAFTA tribunal, after hearing appeals from two U.S. state court decisions, upheld a Massachusetts court decision and overturned a Mississippi court decision. These judgments cannot be appealed. The American serving on this tribunal, Abner Mikva (a former activist federal judge and U.S. Representative) commented: "If Congress had known that there was anything like this in NAFTA, they would never have voted for it." The part of NAFTA that created this tribunal, chapter 11, received scant attention when NAFTA was passed in 1993.

The NAFTA advocates are planning to expand NAFTA (a three-nation agreement: the U.S., Canada and Mexico) into FTAA (Free Trade Area of the Americas: a thirty-four–nation agreement). The European Union experience shows that economic integration leads to political integration, a loss of national sovereignty and self-government, and submission to the rule of unelected bureaucrats and judges.

The justices' use of foreign sources has encouraged liberal politicians to appeal to foreign tribunals to change the U.S. Constitution. Eleanor Holmes Norton, the Washington, D.C., delegate to Congress, wants foreign authorities to overturn the clause in Article I, Section 8 that authorizes Congress to govern the District of Columbia. She has appealed to the Helsinki Commission to enforce a ruling of the Organization of American States (OAS), which previously ruled that this paragraph violates the American Declaration of the Rights and Duties of Man (the governing charter of the OAS).

When John G. Roberts was questioned during his confirmation hearings, he properly replied that reliance on foreign law is a "misuse of precedent" that wrongly "expands the discretion of the judge" and substitutes a judge's "personal preferences" for the Constitution. It's time for the American people and Congress to make it clear to all judges that it is their duty to base their decisions on the U.S. Constitution, and that it is a violation of their oath of office to base decisions on foreign decisions or practices.

Judges Threaten Property Rights

THE FIFTH AMENDMENT to the U.S. Constitution states, "Nor shall private property be taken for public use without just compensation." This is known as the Takings Clause. That provision, along with similar provisions in state constitutions, protects property owners against the government's seizing their land, homes, and businesses, unless the taking is to serve a "public use" and the property owners are appropriately compensated. The government's power to take private property is known as the power of *eminent domain*.

"Public use" has the same plain meaning today as it did when the Constitution was written. Legitimate public uses include constructing a city hall or a courthouse, or building a highway or public transportation system. In all cases, government must pay just compensation to the property owner. In practice, such payment is often far less than the economic loss and inconvenience, but the "public use" limitation should mean that takings are relatively rare.

Never did our Founders anticipate that government would take private property away from Peter to give to Paul. America is a land of limited government, and we have never—except for public use—given our elected officials the power to take away our homes and businesses and turn them over to other citizens or businesses likely to generate more taxes from the property, or who may have better political connections. As John Adams wrote: "The moment the idea is admitted into society, that property is not as sacred as the laws of God, and that there is not a force of law and public justice to protect it, anarchy and tyranny commence. If 'Thou shalt not covet,' and 'Thou shalt not steal,' were not commandments of Heaven, they must be made inviolable precepts in every society, before it can be civilized or made free."

For 165 years, our courts faithfully enforced the Takings Clause the way it was written. The U.S. Supreme Court declared in 1798 in *Calder v. Bull* that "a law that takes property from A. and gives it to B: It is against all reason and justice, for a people to entrust a Legislature with such powers; and, therefore, it cannot be presumed that they have done it."

In 1896 in *Missouri Pacific Railway Co. v. Nebraska*, the Supreme Court held that the "taking by a State of the private property of one person or corporation, without the owner's consent, for the private use of another, is not due process of law, and is a violation of the Fourteenth Article of Amendment of the Constitution of the United States."

In 1905, in *Madisonville Traction Co. v. St. Bernard Mining Co.*, the Court again held that it is "fundamental in American jurisprudence that private property cannot be taken by the Government, National or state, except for purposes which are of a public character, although such taking be accompanied by compensation to the owner. That principle, this court has said, grows out of the essential nature of all free governments."

As late as 1930, we could rely on the Supreme Court to uphold private property. In *Cincinnati v. Vester*, the Court again held that "the excess condemnation was in violation of the constitutional rights of the plaintiffs upon the ground that it was not a taking for a public use within the meaning of that term as it heretofore has been held to justify the taking of private property."

THE WARREN COURT

Then came the Warren Court with its unconstitutional notions that it could reinterpret the U.S. Constitution, change its words, redefine them, and invent new law.

In its very first term, the Warren Court in 1954 rewrote the Fifth Amendment. Justice William O. Douglas changed the words "public use" to "public interest" or "public purpose." That case, *Berman v. Parker*, considered a challenge to a federal program to take private property in the District of Columbia and hand it over to other private parties for redevelopment. Congress had passed the District of Columbia Redevelopment Act of 1945, which authorized the taking of "blighted" property.

The government tested the limits of that statute by seizing property that was not blighted as well as property that was. One piece of property housed a department store at 712 Fourth Street, sw. The Supreme Court admitted that this parcel was "commercial, not residential property; it is not slum housing; it will be put into the project under the management of a private, not a public, agency and redeveloped for private, not public, use."

The owner sued to protect his private property against the government's taking. The trial court ruled that government could condemn property only to advance slum clearance, and limited the definition of a slum to conditions "injurious to the public health, safety, morals and welfare." Not all the property in the case could be labeled a "slum."

But the Warren Court discarded the centuries-old rule that government should take private property only for a bona fide public use. Instead, the Court declared that "once the question of the public purpose has been decided, the amount and character of land to be taken for the project and the need for a particular tract to complete the integrated plan rests in the discretion of the legislative branch."

The Warren Court tried to conceal its mischief by making it appear that it was deferring to the wishes of the legislative branch. In fact, the justices were rewriting the Constitution and thereby depriving property owners of their rightful protection. The *Berman* decision was based on liberal dogma that the government can fix any problem. "The experts" had concluded, Justice Douglas ruled, that "it was important to redesign the whole area" rather than allow "the piecemeal approach."

But our Bill of Rights was written to protect piecemeal individual rights. It does not authorize government to plan our lives and property. The *Berman* decision started a trend of aggressive takings nationwide. All over the country, social-engineering projects replaced settled neighborhoods with concrete and vacant lots.

State court judges began to think that if the Supreme Court could get by with supremacist decisions, they could, too. Relying on the Supreme Court's *Berman* decision, the Michigan Supreme Court in 1981 in *Poletown Neighborhood Council v. Detroit* upheld the shocking seizure of hundreds of businesses, more than a thousand homes, and even several churches in the Polish community in Detroit known as Poletown, for the benefit of General Motors. Steamrollers razed all those businesses, homes and churches for the alleged "public benefit" of building a new General Motors factory.

Inspired by this raw display of government power, similar takings from some persons to give to others proceeded all over the country. *Poletown* became the decision that state courts, city councils and big development corporations loved to cite.

The American Dream is to start a small business and develop it through years of hard work and investment. Millions of small businesses form the backbone of our economy, annually creating 60 to 80 percent of all new jobs.

Location is the key to most businesses, and entrepreneurs typically build their reputation at a particular spot. A lifetime of effort can be suddenly undone by the arbitrary decision of a few councilmen or unelected city planners. The business owner can claim only an appraised value for the hollow building and land that he actually owns, and in most states he receives zero for the goodwill and revenue stream from customers he has nourished over the years. A business leasing its property usually receives no compensation, and the employees get nothing.

Sometimes, a town announces a massive plan to seize properties for development long before it can become a reality. That depresses actual and appraised property values, thereby reducing the price the property owners will receive.

Eminent domain has become a way for politically connected developers to enrich themselves at the expense of small businesses and homeowners. More and more frequently, local governments have used such concepts as "blight" and "economic development" as excuses to destroy thriving private businesses and homes in order to pave the way for wealthy developers to build new big-box shopping centers or theme parks. This makes the large developers very happy; they get a big new shopping center at a bargain-basement price. This process makes the cities happy; cities often receive increased sales- and property-tax revenue. The losers are the former homeowners and businesses.

The familiar argument that eminent domain takings for private development are necessary for slum clearance or removing blighted areas is not supported by experience. Even when areas are blighted, consensual property acquisition is the better solution and has been successful in many areas.

REWRITING THE CONSTITUTION—AGAIN

Those who believe in the U.S. Constitution as it was written and in the right of private property began to hope that the Supreme Court would remedy the long series of mistaken decisions, and the injustices they have caused, by a new decision in a case coming out of New London, Connecticut.

But the people's hopes were dashed. In 2005, the Supreme Court opted for judicial supremacy rather than the U.S. Constitution. In one of its final decisions of the term, the Court fully embraced its own rewriting of the Constitution's words "public use" into the judicially created words "public purpose." The Court then defined "public purpose" to include the alleged public benefit of increasing the tax flow to government.

In the much-anticipated case of *Kelo v. New London*, Justice Stevens wrote for the 5 to 4 majority that whenever a taking "serves a public purpose" (which can simply mean higher tax revenues for the town), "the takings . . . satisfy the public use requirement of the Fifth Amendment."

Wilhelmina Dery lost the home that she had lived in since she was born there in 1918. Susette Kelo, the lead plaintiff, lost the substantial improvements she made to her house, which will be demolished. The Court conceded in *Kelo v. New London* that compensation is often inadequate for the owner of the seized property, but declared that issue to be outside of the scope of the case.

Justice O'Connor, in perhaps the most bitter dissent of her career, wrote: "Today the Court abandons this long-held, basic limitation on government power. Under the banner of economic development, all private property is now vulnerable to being taken and transferred to another private owner, so long as it might be upgraded. . . . Nothing is to prevent the state from replacing any Motel 6 with a Ritz-Carlton, any home with a shopping mall or any farm with a factory."

The judicial supremacists had struck again. As Justice Thomas wrote in his brilliant dissent, "Something has gone seriously awry with this Court's interpretation of the Constitution. . . . The Court has erased the Public Use Clause from our Constitution."

Justice Thomas's dissent emphasized the importance of the original meaning of the Constitution: "When faced with a clash of constitutional principle and a line of unreasoned cases wholly divorced from the text, history, and structure of our founding document, we should not hesitate to resolve the tension in favor of the Constitution's original meaning." But five justices rejected the Constitution's meaning and substituted their own social views. They rewrote the Fifth Amendment to allow takings for any broadly defined "public purpose," rather than applying the Constitution's express limitation of "public use."

The *Kelo* decision showed that putting more tax dollars in the hands of government ranks higher in liberal priorities than compassion for the minorities they brag about helping. Justice Thomas pointed out in his dissent that "Of all the families displaced by urban renewal from 1949 through 1963, 63 percent of those whose race was known were nonwhite

. . . . Over 97 percent of the individuals forcibly removed from their homes by the slum-clearance project upheld by this Court in *Berman* were black."

Public outrage at the *Kelo* decision came from all sides of the political spectrum and at all levels of government. State legislatures were spurred into action by the public outcry against the Supreme Court's attack on property rights, and about half the states proposed statutes or state constitutional amendments to restrict local governments' eminent-domain powers.

On November 4, 2005, the House of Representatives passed the Private Property Rights Protection Act by a vote of 376 to 38. The bill would deny federal economic development funds to any unit of government that exercises its power of eminent domain for economic development rather than for public use. The bill gives a private cause of action to anyone injured by a violation of this act. The bill moved to the Senate, which had already passed an amendment to the Treasury, Transportation, and HUD appropriations bill, stating that no funds provided in the bill may be used to support any federal, state, or local project that uses the power of eminent domain unless it is used only for a public use.

~ 6 ~

Judges Promote Pornography

J UDICIAL SUPREMACISTS ARE TO BLAME for allowing a torrent of obscenity to engulf the movies, television, the theater, books, and even classroom curricula. Robert Bork observes that "the suffocating vulgarity of popular culture is in large measure the work of the Court. The Court did not create vulgarity, but it defeated attempts of communities to contain and minimize vulgarity."

The Court's virulent judicial activism repeatedly and aggressively defeats the people's attempt to maintain a decent society. The courts stole the legislative function in violation of the separation of powers. The courts have used the First Amendment to carry out a massive attack on public decency.

It wasn't always so. Many Americans can remember when movies contained no obscenity or even profanity. The high level of sex, violence, and profanity in movies started during the era of the Warren Court.

The core of the First Amendment's speech clause is the protection of political speech and, as late as 1942, a unanimous Supreme Court ruled in *Chaplinsky v. New Hampshire* that prohibiting obscene, profane, or insulting words was never thought to raise any constitutional problem because those utterances are not political speech. Now, the Court limits political speech in campaigns and religious speech in schools, but elevates pornography and other assaults on decency to the level of a First Amendment right.

In the landmark case on obscenity, *Roth v. United States* (1957), the Supreme Court ruled: "Implicit in the history of the First Amendment is the rejection of obscenity as utterly without redeeming social importance. . . . We hold that obscenity is not within the constitutionally protected speech or press." *Roth* meant that obscenity has no redeeming social importance whatsoever and is not protected by the First Amendment. A pudding that contains arsenic has no nutritional value.

One of the highly paid lawyers for the smut publishing industry, Charles Rembar, bragged in his book *The End of Obscenity* that he gave the activist judges on the Supreme Court the rationale to reverse convictions under state laws until they were no longer enforceable against obscenity. As the lawyer for *A Book Named "John Cleland's Memoirs of a Woman of Pleasure" v. Massachusetts* (1966), known as the *Fanny Hill* case, Rembar persuaded the Court to make two subtle changes in *Roth*'s language which looked minor at the time, but which wiped out the laws against obscenity.

The Court changed *Roth*'s "social importance" to *Fanny Hill*'s "social value," and transposed the word "utterly" to another part of the sentence. With that bit of semantic chicanery in *Fanny Hill*, the new rule became "A work cannot be proscribed unless it is found to be utterly without social value." The book *Fanny Hill* was held not to be obscene because the prostitute reformed on the last pages of the book.

"Social value" quickly became a password to pornography; all a smut peddler had to do was to insert a few social or literary passages, and his obscenity was clothed with the Constitution. The obscene Swedish movie *I Am Curious—Yellow* was defended on the ground that although it pictured intercourse explicitly and in public, it was protected by the First Amendment because the couple did their act on the balustrade of the royal palace in Stockholm as a protest against social institutions.

After the *Fanny Hill* decision, the pornographers increased the volume of their output many times over—and they matched it with lavish funds for legal talent to carry dozens of cases to the Supreme Court and overwhelm the justices with their sophisticated arguments.

By October 1966, the obscenity racket was in full swing. The dealers flooded the Supreme Court with twenty-six appeals from lower court convictions. The mere existence of twenty-six cases on one subject at one time shows the great financial resources of the obscenity industry, its determination to change our laws that had been in existence for nearly two hundred years, and its optimism that this could be accomplished by the Warren Court with activist liberal justices Earl Warren, William Brennan (who wrote the *Fanny Hill* opinion), Abe Fortas (who had represented pornographers before he went on the Court), Hugo Black, and William O. Douglas adopting the pornographers' most extreme arguments.

The obscenity dealers were not disappointed. From 1966 to 1970, the Warren Court handed down a truly revolutionary series of thirty-four decisions that turned the law of obscenity upside down. These decisions gave extraordinary victories to the pornographers, reversing all the judges, juries, appellate courts, and law enforcement officials connected with those cases. Those thirty-four reversals made laws against obscenity almost impossible to enforce, thereby drastically lowering community decency standards throughout America. (See Notes for a list of these cases.)

All those thirty-four decisions were per curiam (by the Court), making them a major legacy of the Warren Court. More significantly, all thirty-four decisions were anonymous; no justice had the nerve to put his name on any of the decisions. Most of these decisions were only a sentence or two, an unusual tactic which enabled the Court to conceal from public debate the substance of what the Court was approving. One has to search out the lower court decisions to see what gross obscenities the Court was wrapping in the First Amendment.

Typical of these thirty-four anonymous, short, pro-pornography Supreme Court opinions is *Mazes v. Ohio* (1967), which reversed the decisions of the Ohio supreme court, the Ohio court of appeals, the trial judge, and a jury in one sentence: "The petition for a writ of certiorari is granted and the judgment of the Supreme Court of Ohio is reversed. *Redrup v. New York*, 386 U.S. 767."

That is the entire unsigned Supreme Court opinion. The Court couldn't defend the obscenity it was clothing in the First Amendment. *Mazes v. Ohio* entailed the conviction of a merchant for displaying in his open racks *The Orgy Club* in the midst of other obscene works. The Ohio supreme court had noted that "the obscene material found between the covers, viewed from any standpoint, is utterly without redeeming social value," and the arresting officer testified that "there were several young boys in the store" looking at the rack. The Court's silence about the facts of the case tended to obscure the enormity of its transformation of our laws protecting Americans against obscenity.

Hollywood got the message from the Supreme Court. In 1966, the Motion Picture Association of America stopped enforcing its old Production Code, which Hollywood studios had imposed on themselves since 1930. In 1968, the Association's president, Jack Valenti, proudly declared that movie makers were now free "to tell their stories as they choose to tell them."

This new freedom brought obscene language, near-total nudity, graphic sex scenes, and sadistic violence to neighborhood movie theaters. The abrupt change was reflected in the Academy Awards. In 1965, the Best Picture was *The Sound of Music*; in 1969, the Best Picture was *Midnight Cowboy*, an x-rated film about a homeless male hustler.

SUFFOCATING VULGARITY CONTINUES

Those Warren Court decisions completely changed pornography law in America, and some lower federal courts are now even more extreme than the Supreme Court. The evil fruits of the Supreme Court's endorsement of pornography as a First Amendment right are everywhere apparent, and the pro-pornography bias of the federal courts continues to this day.

In a 2 to 1 ruling in *Finley v. National Endowment for the Arts* (1996), the Ninth Circuit U.S. Court of Appeals held that it is unconstitutional for a government agency to consider "decency and respect" for American values when it doles out the taxpayers' money. The winners in this case were Karen Finley (the woman who became famous by parading on stage dressed in nothing but a layer of chocolate), three others whose nude performances centered on homosexual themes, and, of course, the ACLU. The losers were the American taxpayers. Too late to make any difference in the funding, the Supreme Court reversed this decision in 1998.

Another federal judge ruled that *Penthouse* magazine and other sexually explicit magazines and videos have a First Amendment right to be available in subsidized stores on military bases. By the ruling in *General Media Communications v. Perry* (1997), the military was enjoined from obeying the Military Honor and Decency Act of 1996, which forbade such materials on military bases. This was too outrageous for the Second Circuit U.S. Court of Appeals, which reversed, declaring the Act a reasonable regulation of speech in a non-public forum.

Continuing its campaign of using the First Amendment to protect pornographers, the Supreme Court in 2000 struck down a federal statute that required cable operators to stop sending unwanted and never-requested pornographic images into the homes of subscribers during daytime hours (*U.S. v. Playboy Entertainment Group*).

In 2002, the judicial supremacists invalidated half of the Child Pornography Prevention Act of 1996, despite the fact that it had passed Congress with overwhelming majorities and was signed by Bill Clinton (*Ashcroft v. Free Speech Coalition*). This decision knocked out Congress's ban on computer-generated child pornographic images even before the law had a chance to be enforced. Justice Kennedy spent part of his opinion reassuring Hollywood that the Court would never put any limits on the gross sex and violence in current movies.

The following year, the Court nearly invalidated the Children's Internet Protection Act of 1999 based merely on the possibility that adult patrons of public library internet terminals might be inconvenienced by having to ask a librarian to turn off the pornography filter installed to protect children. This decision assured adults that they can continue to enjoy pornography at taxpayers' expense at their local public libraries (*U.S. v. American Library Association*, 2003).

"THE END OF ALL MORALS LEGISLATION"

In 2004, the Supreme Court invalidated the Child Online Protection Act, which banned the posting for "commercial purposes" on the World Wide Web of material that is "patently offensive" in a sexual manner unless the poster takes reasonable steps to restrict access by minors. The law was badly needed, as filth plagues the internet, incites sex crimes, and entraps children. Minors are an intended audience for the highly profitable sex industry. This law did not censor a single word or picture. It merely required the purveyors of sex-for-profit to screen their websites from minors, which can be done by credit card or other verification.

But decency lost again in 2004 when five justices knocked out this new law in *Ashcroft v. ACLU*. Justice Kennedy declared it unconstitutional for Congress to do almost anything to stop porn flowing to teens. He shifted the burden to families to screen out the graphic sex rather than imposing the cost on the companies profiting from the porn. His reasoning is as absurd as telling a family just to pull down its window shades if it doesn't want to see people exposing themselves in the street.

The next blow against decency came in Washington State, where a federal judge wrapped the First Amendment around video and computer games that show teenagers how to kill policemen. The state legislature had imposed a fine on the sale or rental to minors of video or computer games containing "realistic or photographic-like depictions of aggressive conflict in which the player kills, injures, or otherwise causes physical harm to a human form in the game who is depicted . . . as a public law enforcement officer."

Determined to overturn the new law, the Video Software Dealers Association sought out an activist judge who would bend the First Amendment to cover these videos. The dealers found their man in a federal district court judge appointed by President Clinton, Robert S. Lasnik.

In *Video Software Dealers Association v. Maleng* (2004), Judge Lasnik nullified the state statute and prohibited its enforcement. He admitted that the videos are "filth," yet insisted that the First Amendment safeguards them. Judge Lasnik went overboard in his extreme defense of violent video games. He said: "Whether we believe the advent of violent video games adds anything of value to society is irrelevant; guided by the First Amendment, we are obliged to recognize that they are as much entitled to the protection of free speech as the best of literature." So a video showing how to kill policemen deserves the same constitutional protection as Shakespeare and Herman Melville.

The 1996 Ensign Amendment prohibited the use of federal funds by the U.S. Bureau of Prisons to "distribute or make available any commercially published information or material to a prisoner . . . [when] such information or material is sexually explicit or features nudity." That surely sounds like a reasonable and necessary law because criminals are in jail for punishment, not to pursue vices partly at our expense.

Three judges on the Court of Appeals for the Third Circuit overturned the Ensign ban on porn for prisoners and held in favor of pornography in *Ramirez v. Pugh* (2004). The judges said the law was too broad in that it denied pornography to prisoners who had not been convicted of sex-related crimes. But prisons are maintained by our tax dollars, and only Congress is authorized to make spending decisions. The idea of the taxpayers having to pay for distribution of pornography to prisoners, no matter what they are convicted of, is ridiculous. This is one more example of supremacist judges telling us how we must spend our own money.

Just when we thought the pro-pornography bias of the federal courts couldn't get any worse, it did. In 2005, another Clinton-appointed judge essentially declared federal obscenity laws to be unconstitutional and unenforceable. In *U.S. v. Extreme Associates*, he threw out an indictment against defendants who sold material over the internet which all sides agreed was obscene.

U.S. District Judge Gary Lancaster explained that his decision was a result of *Lawrence v. Texas* (2003), the sodomy case: "The *Lawrence* decision, however, is nevertheless important to this case. It can be reasonably interpreted as holding that public morality is not a legitimate state interest sufficient to justify infringing on adult, private, consensual, sexual conduct even if that conduct is deemed offensive to the general public's sense of morality. Such is the import of *Lawrence* to our decision." Justice Scalia's dissent in *Lawrence* was prophetic: "This effectively decrees the end of all morals legislation."

The Third Circuit overturned the *Extreme Associates* ruling, but it stands as an example of the pro-pornography bias of many life-tenured judges and of the continuing mischief of *Lawrence v. Texas*.

The pornographic sea continues to rise in Hollywood movies, and even daily newspapers complain about the "ratings creep" that allows more and more violent and sexually explicit content.

Although the public won't patronize x-rated movies in respectable movie theaters, the x-rated and xxx-rated video business has become a multi-billion-dollar industry, turning out about four thousand movies a year under protection of the First Amendment as defined by the Supreme Court.

The courts are not *interpreting* the First Amendment; they are *rewriting* it to guarantee the profits of pornographers. The judicial supremacists have made the First Amendment a traffic signal that flashes green to pornographers but red or yellow to religious and political speech. From Hollywood movies, to primetime and cable television, to dirty books and songs, "the suffocating vulgarity of popular culture" is all around us.

We can't hope for any revival of civility and morality in the entertainment industry until Congress clips the power of the Imperial Judiciary to overturn legislative attempts to maintain decency.

～ 7 ～

Judges Foster Feminism

ABORTION LAW had traditionally been in the domain of the states, as was nearly all criminal law. Beginning in 1967, seventeen states weakened their anti-abortion laws in various ways. The tide turned against abortion in 1970, as pro-abortion bills were introduced and defeated in thirty-three states. Even the New York legislature repealed its two-year-old abortion-on-demand law (only to have the repeal vetoed by Governor Nelson Rockefeller). On November 7, 1972, pro-abortion referenda were defeated in North Dakota by 78 percent and in Michigan by 61 percent.

Then, on January 22, 1973, the U.S. Supreme Court—in the preeminent act of judicial supremacy of our time—struck down the abortion laws of all fifty states.

The core holding of *Roe v. Wade* is widely misunderstood. It is commonly described in terms of viability or trimesters, or as allowing state regulation under some circumstances.

On the contrary, *Roe v. Wade* held that a woman has an unrestricted right to abortion at any time during the entire nine months of her pregnancy, provided it is deemed medically necessary to preserve her life or health. The term "medically necessary" was defined to mean that a doctor has agreed to perform the abortion—and this decision need not be justified. The term "health" was defined in the companion case decided the same day, *Doe v. Bolton*, to include "all factors—physical, emotional, psychological, familial, and the woman's age—relevant to the well-being of the patient." The practical consequence is that any doctor can perform an abortion at any time.

Roe v. Wade was an outrageous creation of the judicial supremacists. This decision grabbed a legislative function away from the state legislatures and imposed a judicial fiat without any textual basis in the U.S. Constitution. As Justice Byron White said in dissent, *Roe v. Wade* was "an exercise of raw judicial power." He wrote, "I find nothing in the language or history of the Constitution to support the Court's judgment. The Court simply fashions and announces a new constitutional right . . . ."

Justice Rehnquist explained further that the decision "partakes more of judicial legislation than it does of a determination of the intent of the drafters of the Fourteenth Amendment . . . To reach its result the Court necessarily has had to find within the scope of the Fourteenth Amendment a right that was apparently completely unknown to the drafters of the Amendment."

Justice William O. Douglas's confidential papers, which were made available by the Library of Congress in 1988, revealed that the justices were shamelessly plotting with each other to achieve the predetermined result of legalized abortion.

Roe v. Wade was an extraordinary exercise of judicial supremacy and was the godmother to a whole series of subsequent decisions on many subjects for which no basis exists in the Constitution. *Roe v. Wade* is a prime example of the judicial supremacists playing the wildcard of substantive due process.

Supreme Court arrogance reached new heights in *Planned Parenthood v. Casey* (1992), when the Court linked its own legitimacy with abortion in a circular argument. Although *Roe v. Wade* had no basis in the Constitution, the Court in *Casey* urged that *Roe* be cast in stone lest "the Court's legitimacy be undermined." In other words, in order to maintain the Court's legitimacy, we must not criticize an illegitimate decision. Neither *Roe* nor *Casey* was based on any plausible reading of the U.S. Constitution.

The feminists now try to make all federal court nominees promise they will never overturn *Roe v. Wade*, usually demanding that they proclaim their fidelity to "settled law" and to *stare decisis* (stand by the decision).

But how about asking nominees these questions: Do you believe juvenile capital punishment was "settled law" in *Stanford v. Kentucky* (1989)? Do you think the Supreme Court made a mistake in overturning it in *Roper v. Simmons* only sixteen years later? Do you believe state anti-sodomy laws were settled law in *Bowers v. Hardwick* (1986)—so do you think the Supreme Court made a mistake in overturning it in *Lawrence v. Texas* only seventeen years later? Would you have recommended *stare decisis* for the *Dred Scott v. Sanford* and the *Plessy v. Ferguson* decisions—or would you have repudiated *stare decisis*? The Supreme Court has overturned dozens of its own decisions, illustrating how silly it is to demand that nominees pledge fidelity to a controversial ruling.

From 1995 to 2000, laws prohibiting partial-birth abortion were passed by thirty states, usually by overwhelming margins. Within days of each new state law becoming effective, abortion advocates rushed to find an activist federal judge to slap an injunction against enforcement. The Supreme Court knocked out all these laws in *Stenberg v. Carhart* (2000), to the surprise of those who had not realized the full scope of *Roe v. Wade*. In his dissent in *Stenberg*, Justice Thomas wrote: "From reading the majority's sanitized description, one would think that this case involves state regulation of a widely accepted routine medical procedure. Nothing could be further from the truth. The most widely used method of abortion during this stage of pregnancy is so gruesome that its use can be traumatic even for the physicians and medical staff who perform it."

In 2003, Congress concluded that the Supreme Court had acted on faulty premises, and Congress passed a federal partial-birth abortion ban that attempted to conform to the Court's twisted logic. Abortion advocates again persuaded activist judges to overturn the legislation, claiming that this gruesome procedure is medically necessary, but refusing to provide the medical records necessary to test their claim.

PUSHING FOR A GENDER-NEUTRAL SOCIETY

Roe v. Wade is the centerpiece of the feminization of the judiciary. This process was accelerated by the elevation to the Supreme Court of two women, neither of whom was questioned during her confirmation hearing about her extensive paper trail of feminist extremism.

Ruth Bader Ginsburg won early acclaim from the feminists because of her role as the attorney who wrote the amicus curiae brief which the ACLU filed in the 1973 Supreme Court case of *Frontiero v. Richardson*, one of the first attempts to get activist judges to rewrite U.S. laws in conformity with feminist ideology. Justice William Brennan's majority opinion articulated the feminist nonsense that American men, "in practical effect, put women, not on a pedestal, but in a cage," and "throughout much of the 19th century the position of women in our society was, in many respects, comparable to that of blacks under the pre-Civil War slave codes."

Anyone who thinks that free American women were ever treated like slaves or kept in a cage has a worldview that is a dangerous basis for Supreme Court decisions. Brennan is no longer on the Court, but we do have his soulmate, Ginsburg, who subscribes to the same fantasies and praised *Frontiero* as an "activist" decision.

Before Ruth Bader Ginsburg was nominated for the Supreme Court by President Clinton, she authored a book, *Sex Bias in the U.S. Code,* supporting the proposed federal Equal Rights Amendment. In that book, she advocated not only assigning women to military combat duty, but affirmative action for women in the military, sex-integrating everything from prisons to the Boy Scouts, and even changing 750 federal laws to censor all male nouns and pronouns because they allegedly discriminate against women.

Justice Ginsburg has long been on record as wanting cases to be decided on what she calls "the equality principle" (rather than on the Constitution). In her 1980 book, *Constitutional Government in America*, she endorsed taxpayer funding of abortions as a constitutional right (something that even the pro-*Roe v. Wade* Supreme Court rejected in *Harris v. McRae* in 1980).

When Ginsburg stood beside President Clinton in the Rose Garden the day he nominated her for the Supreme Court, she said she wished that her mother had "lived in an age when daughters are cherished as much as sons." Where did her mother live—in China? Her statement was an insult to all American parents who do, indeed, cherish their daughters as much as their sons.

After she joined the Supreme Court, Ginsburg's major effort to aid the feminists' campaign to plunge us into a gender-neutral society was her sudden discovery in 1996 of a new entitlement for women to enroll at the Virginia Military Institute, a privilege nobody else had detected during VMI's previous 157 years. She wrote the Court's opinion in *United States v. Virginia* ordering women to be admitted to Virginia Military Institute, and even smeared as "close-minded" those who believe there are inherent differences between men and women. Without any authority from the

Constitution, Ginsburg led the Court into pandering to
the feminist prejudice against the type of masculinity that
was typical of VMI.

Ginsburg's feminist influence on other justices is seen in
a 2003 decision that shocked observers, *Nevada Department
of Human Resources v. Hibbs*. She didn't write the decision,
but the feminist phraseology is unmistakably hers. The
Court's tirade against "stereotypes" (a word used eighteen
times), which supposedly "forced women to continue
to assume the role of primary family caregiver," echoes
Ginsburg's prejudice against the concept of "breadwinning
husband" and "dependent, homemaking wife," which she
had expressed in *Sex Bias in the U.S. Code*. "Stereotyping" is
a favorite *bête noire* of the feminists and often refers to the
traditional view that children are best raised by a mother
and father who are married to each other.

Ginsburg makes no secret of her continued close ties
with the pro-abortion feminists. She lends her name and
presence to a lecture series sponsored by the NOW Legal
Defense and Education Fund, a feminist advocacy group
that often files amicus briefs in support of feminist causes.
Thirteen members of Congress have asked her to withdraw
from cases having to do with abortion because of these ties,
but she has refused.

The feminization of the judiciary led the federal courts
to micromanage the athletic teams at Brown, a private university. A national leader in offering athletic opportunities
to women, Brown made a budgetary decision to recast two
men's and two women's sports teams as "intercollegiate"

rather than "varsity," a change that affected more men than women.

But the feminists filed a class action lawsuit claiming sex discrimination under Title IX. Litigation spanned ten years and cost Brown over one million dollars in compelled payment of plaintiffs' attorney's fees. The courts ordered Brown to restore full funding for the two women's teams, though not the men's teams (*Cohen v. Brown University*, 1992 through 2003).

THE STEREOTYPICAL WOMAN

The other woman on the Supreme Court, Sandra Day O'Connor, had a record of feminist extremism similar to Ginsburg's, and both women got a free pass in their confirmation hearings from the chivalrous men on the Senate Judiciary Committee.

O'Connor had served on a tax-funded feminist commission called the Defense Advisory Committee On Women In The Services (DACOWITS). The minutes of this group show that O'Connor "initiated" the discussion and made the motion in the Utilization Subcommittee in April 1975 urging Congress to repeal the laws that exempt women from military combat duty. Her motion was passed in the full DACOWITS year after year and resulted in a House hearing in 1979 where, fortunately, wiser men killed the proposed legislation. Assigning women to military combat duty is a priority item on the feminist agenda to propel us into a gender-neutral society.

With her feminist background, it was no surprise that O'Connor twice voted to keep abortion legal (in *Planned Parenthood v. Casey* and *Stenberg v. Carhart*) and twice voted for gay rights (in *Romer v. Evans* and *Lawrence v. Texas*). As a member of the Arizona Legislature, she voted repeatedly for pro-abortion bills, and she co-sponsored ratification of the federal Equal Rights Amendment (which Arizona refused to ratify).

The feminization of the Court has played a major factor in creating the problem of judicial supremacy. Numerous decisions for which O'Connor has been the swing vote have had an insidious effect. She is the judicial personification of the stereotype that a woman will change her mind, be unpredictable, and make decisions that are inconsistent and unfathomable to rational men.

Elevated to the Court by President Reagan, she positioned herself as the ultimate centrist whose opinions cannot be predicted because they blow with the wind and follow no logical pattern. Since the Supreme Court is split between liberals and conservatives, O'Connor became the deciding vote in many important cases, allowing the liberal media to call her the most powerful woman in America. She is credited with being the deciding vote in many 5 to 4 decisions on major issues of public policy, including abortion (*Planned Parenthood v. Casey*, 1992), partial-birth abortion (*Stenberg v. Carhart*, 2000), vouchers to religious schools (*Zelman v. Simmons-Harris*, 2002), racial preferences in university admissions (*Grutter v. Bollinger*, 2003), and campaign finance reform (*McConnell v. FEC*, 2003).

Justice O'Connor provided the decisive fifth vote in 2005 to force county courthouses to tear down displays of the Ten Commandments (*McCreary County v. ACLU of Kentucky*). O'Connor supposedly supports state power and opposes federal interference, but on the important issues of religion and abortion she repeatedly favored federal intervention to advance her unpopular views.

Lacking any consistent ideology or respect for the separation of powers, O'Connor claims to base her rulings on such nebulous and equivocal "tests" as "undue burden," "an appearance of endorsement," or "a reasonable observer."

The problem with these 5 to 4 decisions is not that they are close calls, but that under the current regime of judicial supremacy, in which the legal community accepts a 5 to 4 decision as the law of the land, all these issues will be constantly re-litigated because no one can predict how similar cases will be decided. Nobody knows what the law is; it depends on the whim of the swing justice.

The legal community continues to propagate the unconstitutional notion that the Constitution is whatever the Supreme Court says it is, but are less and less confident of what the Supreme Court will say. The result is that Justice O'Connor is responsible for concentrating more and more power in the Supreme Court to resolve intricate matters of public policy.

O'Connor's devotion to judicial supremacy was made clear by her opinion in *Planned Parenthood v. Casey*: "So, indeed, must be the character of a Nation of people who aspire to live according to the rule of law. Their belief in themselves as such a people is not readily separable from their understanding of the Court invested with the authority to decide their constitutional cases and speak before all others for their constitutional ideals."

She claims our "belief" in "the rule of law" requires us to accept a Court "invested with the authority" above "all others" to decide what are our "constitutional ideals." She wants the rule of law to require Americans to allow the Supreme Court to be the sole interpreter of the Constitution even if that means upholding an obviously wrong decision.

The truth is just the opposite. We are not living under the rule of law so long as unaccountable judges are allowed to exercise the sole authority to invent new and contrary interpretations of the Constitution and of laws passed by our elected representatives. That is rule by an oligarchy of judges, not the rule of law.

We hope some day we will have a woman on the Supreme Court who is a real judge, not a feminist or a politician. Republican presidents cannot afford another O'Connor.

~ 8 ~

Judges Handicap
Law Enforcement

SUPREME COURT JUSTICES seem to think that criminals need protection from the police.

The Warren Court rewrote criminal law and police procedures in a series of cases, starting with *Escobedo v. State of Illinois* (1964), which dissenting Justice Stewart wrote "... frustrates the vital interests of society in preserving the legitimate and proper function of honest and purposeful police investigation."

The most famous Warren Court interference with law enforcement was *Miranda v. Arizona* (1966). The *Miranda* warning doesn't seem so radical today, but it was at the time, and *Miranda* was then applied in a radical way to cripple law enforcement.

Consider the 1968 Iowa case of Robert Anthony Williams, who was arrested in connection with the disappearance of a young girl. He invoked his right to a lawyer, and while a couple of police officers were driving him to see his lawyer, one policeman spoke what became known as the "Christian burial speech":

> I want to give you something to think about while we're traveling down the road. . . . Number one, I want you to observe the weather conditions, it's raining, it's sleeting, it's freezing, driving is very treacherous, visibility is poor, it's going to be dark early this evening. They are predicting several inches of snow for tonight, and I feel that you yourself are the only person that knows where this little girl's body is, that you yourself have only been there once, and if you get a snow on top of it you yourself may be unable to find it. And, since we will be going right past the area on the way into Des Moines, I felt that we could stop and locate the body, and that the parents of this little girl should be entitled to a Christian burial for the little girl who was snatched away from them on Christmas Eve and murdered. And I feel we should stop and locate it on the way in rather than waiting until morning and trying to come back out after a snowstorm and possibly not being able to find it at all. . . . I do not want you to answer me. I don't want to discuss it any further. Just think about it as we're riding down the road.

Williams subsequently led the police to the little girl's body. The Supreme Court overturned Williams's conviction in *Brewer v. Williams* (1977), saying that the case was tainted by police misconduct and the discovery could not be used as evidence. Nearly everyone else thought the police work was outstanding.

TRYING TO STOP CAPITAL PUNISHMENT

In spite of the fact that the Constitution specifically authorizes capital punishment, in 1972 the Supreme Court threw
out three death penalty convictions in *Furman v. Georgia*,
claiming they were violations of the Eighth and Fourteenth
Amendments. The 5 to 4 decision called on the states to
"rethink" their death penalty laws, effectively knocking out
death penalty laws everywhere and halting all executions.
Furman included two hundred pages of concurrence and
dissent, with Justices Brennan and Thurgood Marshall
arguing that the death penalty is unconstitutional in all
cases.

Apparently the judicial supremacists thought that their
rewriting of the Constitution on capital punishment would
end the matter. But public resolve in favor of retribution for
heinous crimes remained strong, and most states passed new
death penalty laws for first-degree murder with aggravating
circumstances.

In *Atkins v. Virginia* (2002), Justice John Paul Stevens
rewrote the Eighth Amendment to outlaw capital punishment for those with low IQs. Stevens could not base his ruling on the Constitution, since it endorses the death penalty,
so he relied on "evolving standards" and "polling data."

Justice Stevens seems to think that laws can be made
through his interpretation of public opinion polls. Justice
Scalia rebuked him, retorting that *Atkins* was based on
"nothing but the personal views" of the justices.

This ruling threw death penalty enforcement into chaos,
as no one knows what are the IQ requirements for execution,

how and when IQ tests are to be administered, or what are
the procedures for bringing a low-IQ claim. Even if there is
a consensus that low-IQ murderers should not be executed,
these issues should be resolved by the legislature, not by
the courts ad hoc.

In *In re Stanford* (2002), four Supreme Court justices
tried unsuccessfully to persuade a majority to hold that it is
unconstitutional to execute a juvenile. They said: "Scientific
advances such as the use of functional magnetic resonance
imaging—MRI scans—have provided valuable data that
serve to make the case even stronger that adolescents 'are
more vulnerable, more impulsive, and less self-disciplined
than adults.'" MRI scans are very useful for medical diag-
noses, but are not suitable for constitutional diagnosis.

The Court's 5 to 4 decision in *Roper v. Simmons* (2005)
outlawed capital punishment for seventeen-year-olds, taking off death row seventy-two criminals in twelve states
who were under age eighteen when they committed their
crimes. It was an about-face for the Court: it had rejected
the same arguments just sixteen years earlier in *Stanford v.
Kentucky*.

This decision is a prime example of liberal judges
changing our Constitution based on their judge-invented
notion that its meaning is evolving. Justice Anthony Kennedy presumed to rewrite the Eighth Amendment again.
He excused juvenile killers because of "lack of maturity"
and "impetuous" actions.

In fact, Christopher Simmons showed how calculating
a juvenile killer can be. He told friends it would be fun to
commit a burglary and then murder the victim, and he

explained how he would do it, assuring them they could "get away with it" because they were juveniles.

Simmons met his friend at 2 a.m., and they broke into Shirley Crook's home as she slept. Simmons and his fellow teenager bound her hands, covered her eyes and mouth with duct tape, and drove her in her own minivan to a state park. They walked her to a railroad trestle, hog-tied her hands and feet with electrical wire, wrapped her entire face in duct tape, and threw her into the Meramec River where she drowned helplessly. Her body was found later by fishermen.

Showing no remorse, Simmons bragged about the killing, declaring that he did it "because the bitch seen my face." He confessed quickly after his arrest and performed a videotaped reenactment at the crime scene.

A jury of Simmons' peers listened to his attorney's argument that Simmons' age should mitigate punishment. The jury observed Simmons' demeanor at trial and heard from a slew of witnesses. After an exhaustive trial and full consideration of age as a factor, the jury and judge imposed the death sentence as allowed by Missouri law. Nothing in the text or history of the Eighth Amendment denies Missouri juries and state legislatures the power to make this decision.

In dissent, Justice Scalia blasted the "updating" of the Eighth Amendment. He concluded, "The result will be to crown arbitrariness with chaos." The terrorists and the vicious Salvadoran gangs that have invaded our cities will now be able to assign seventeen-year-olds as their hit men so they can "get away with it."

SHELTERED FROM CRITICISM

Some judges arrogantly think they should be sheltered from criticism by the other branches of government. Congress passed an innocuous law asking the Justice Department to report on whether federal criminal sentencing is within the official guidelines. A federal judge in California declared the law unconstitutional (*U.S. v. Mendoza*, 2004) because the dissemination of information might generate criticism of the judiciary. It is ridiculous to think that the Imperial Judiciary may prohibit the legislature from asking the executive branch for some information just because the judiciary might be criticized. Whatever happened to freedom of speech?

House Judiciary Committee Chairman F. James Sensenbrenner Jr. made a blunt speech to the U.S. Judicial Conference on March 16, 2004, regarding congressional oversight of the judiciary:

> In a letter to me dated November 7, 2003 this body (the Judicial Conference of the United States) objected to 'the dissemination of judge-specific data on sentencing in criminal cases,' and suggested that "Congress should meet its responsibility to oversee the functioning of the criminal justice system through use of this data without subjecting individual judges to the risk of unfair criticism in isolated cases."
>
> I have been perplexed as to why such furor has been raised over obtaining records from a judge's publicly decided cases. Assuredly, federal judges in

a democracy may be scrutinized, and may even be "unfairly criticized." Subject to removal from office upon conviction of impeachment, Article III judges have been given lifetime tenure precisely to be better able to withstand such criticism, not to be immune from it. That the Congress, the elected representatives of the people, may obtain and review the public records of the Judicial branch is both Constitutionally authorized and otherwise appropriate. Over 200 years of precedents show that the Judiciary as a collective body, or an individual judge, is subject to Congressional inquiry.

Unfortunately, Congress doesn't very often use its constitutionally authorized power over the judiciary.

~ 9 ~

Judges Invite Illegal Immigration

THE PECULIAR NOTION that foreigners residing illegally in the United States should enjoy the same rights as American citizens is found nowhere in the U.S. Constitution or federal law. This anomaly was created by supremacist judges.

First, the Supreme Court denied government the right to distinguish between citizens and aliens, then encouraged and protected the large-scale entry of illegal aliens into the United States. Holdovers from the Warren Court presumed to mandate this policy even though the Constitution clearly recognizes the basic difference between citizens and aliens. Justice William Rehnquist explained this in his lone dissent in *Sugarman v. Dougall* (1973), a case that overturned New York's requirement that state civil servants be U.S. citizens. Rehnquist wrote that "the Constitution itself recognizes the difference between citizens and aliens. That distinction is constitutionally important in no less than eleven instances in a political document noted for its brevity ."

In 1971, in *Graham v. Richardson*, Justice Harry Blackmun added a new right to the Fourteenth Amendment. Writing for the Court's majority, Blackmun held that "a state statute that denies welfare benefits to resident aliens and one that denies them to aliens who have not resided in the United States for a specified number of years violate the Equal Protection Clause." Grabbing power for judges to override legislative policymaking, Blackmun stated that "classifications based on alienage, like those based on nationality or race, are inherently suspect and subject to close judicial scrutiny."

The Supreme Court continued to blur the distinction between citizens and aliens. In 1973, in *In Re Griffiths*, the Supreme Court ruled that this new equal-protection privilege gives noncitizens the right to take the bar exam and become licensed lawyers.

One would think that government employees should be citizens of the same country as their government. But asserting "judicial scrutiny" in *Hampton v. Mow Sun Wong*, the Supreme Court in 1976 substituted its own views for those of Congress and ruled that citizenship is an unconstitutional requirement for holding a government job.

Justice William Brennan, who was appointed in 1956 but continued to promote judicial supremacy long after Earl Warren retired, was still on the Court in 1982 when he wrote the 5 to 4 decision that opened the floodgates to illegal aliens.

In *Plyler v. Doe*, Brennan created a brand-new addition to the Constitution's equal protection clause: the requirement that the State of Texas must provide free public education to the children of foreigners who had entered the United States illegally. Texas had passed a law limiting public education to those who were in our country lawfully. Justice Brennan and his fellow activists ruled that the Texas law was unconstitutional. They misused the equal protection clause to prohibit any state from denying free education to illegal aliens unless the state proved "some substantial state interest"—and saving the taxpayers' money was deemed to be insufficient justification.

The *Plyler* decision gave foreigners a powerful incentive to sneak into our country: they could enroll their children in our public schools. They could also start demanding other benefits paid for by U.S. taxpayers because of Brennan's broad-brush opinion in *Plyler*. Brennan ruled that because aliens are a "class" of people, they must be treated equally with every other person in the state regardless of the financial cost to the taxpayers. Thus, the Brennan decision opened our borders to a stampede of illegal aliens.

In 2001, the Supreme Court declared that "once an alien enters the country, the legal circumstance changes, for the Due Process Clause applies to all 'persons' within the United States, including aliens, whether their presence here is lawful, unlawful, temporary, or permanent." The Supreme Court created this fiction in *Zadvydas v. Davis*.

The notorious Court of Appeals for the Ninth Circuit, which presides over California, Arizona, and other western states, has driven a truck through this opening created by the Supreme Court. With every new dispute, the Ninth Circuit has sweetened the bait that attracts millions of illegal aliens. "The Fifth Amendment also protects aliens," the Ninth

Circuit declared in *Torres-Aguilar v. INS* (2001). In *Sagana v. Tenorio* (2004), the Ninth Circuit added, "Aliens who are in the jurisdiction of the United States under any status, even as illegal entrants or under a legal fiction, are entitled to the protections of the Fourteenth Amendment."

In 2005, the Ninth Circuit ruled in *Mohammed v. Gonzales* that women from countries that allow female mutilation are eligible for asylum in the United States. Amnesty International estimates that 135 million girls and women, mostly in Africa, are victims of this horrendous practice, and that an additional two million more are currently at risk. The sheer numbers of applicants who could petition for asylum on this basis are mind-boggling.

It is no wonder that the Ninth Circuit has become a mecca for immigration cases. According to Clinton-appointed Ninth Circuit Judge Michael Daly Hawkins, "Three years ago, immigration cases were 8 percent of our calendar. Today, as we speak, that percentage is 48 percent."

MORE INTERFERENCE IN PUBLIC SCHOOLS

More Supreme Court mischief involving immigrants and public schools was started in 1974 by *Lau v. Nichols*, a decision written by yet another Warren Court holdover, William O. Douglas. He refused to relinquish judicial power longer than any Supreme Court justice in history, staying over thirty-six years.

The Civil Rights Act of 1964, Title VI, says that "No person in the United States shall, on the ground of race, color, or national origin, be excluded from participation in, be denied the benefits of, or be subjected to discrimination under any program or activity receiving Federal financial assistance." The law says nothing about language. Legislating from the bench, the Court made two errors. First, it allowed the bureaucracy to twist the definition of "national origin" to include language deficiency. Second, it allowed a private right of action based on this change, such that almost anyone could sue over it. This decision authorized the federal courts to create and enforce the rights of non-English speaking people, thereby taking away power from Congress to decide this issue.

This decision was the origin of the mistake called bilingual education, a system of keeping immigrant children speaking their native language in public schools instead of rapidly learning English. Immigrant children were kept in segregated classrooms for up to 80 percent of the day, often for five to seven years, never learning English. California schools ultimately taught public school children in forty-two different languages.

Prior to the *Lau* decision, the United States had assimilated millions of immigrants over two centuries without the government providing foreign-language teachers. Immigrant children went directly into public schools where only English was spoken. They rapidly learned English and went home and taught it to their parents. After *Lau v. Nichols*, the schools abandoned the system that had proved so successful and substituted bilingual education.

This system of language apartheid grew into a billion-dollar boondoggle and resulted in harm, not benefit, to the children it was supposed to help. Two decades later, the voters in California, Arizona, and Massachusetts passed referenda repudiating bilingual education, but a generation of children had grown up without learning English.

THE CITIZENSHIP CLAUSE AND OATH

The Citizenship Clause of the Fourteenth Amendment states that U.S. citizens are "all persons born or naturalized in the United States and subject to the jurisdiction thereof." Federal law uses almost identical language. "Subject to the jurisdiction thereof" is an essential part of the definition.

History clearly confirms the importance and necessity of those five words. American Indians, despite the obvious location of their birth, did not receive U.S. citizenship until it was conferred by congressional acts in 1887, 1901, and 1924, long after ratification of the Fourteenth Amendment. The extensive litigation concerning American Indians proves that the consent of both the government and the individual is what controls citizenship, rather than place of birth.

What about babies who may be born to diplomats or their wives who happen to be in the United States at the moment of birth? They are not U.S. citizens, either. A baby born to the wife of the ambassador from France, for example, will surely be a French citizen, not an American citizen. Dating back to the Roman Empire, citizenship has always been a privilege extended only on conditions established by the sovereign (as it was granted to St. Paul), not the mere happenstance of location of birth or residence.

For nearly two centuries, the Supreme Court faithfully construed citizenship consistent with the Constitution and the intent of our Founders. In 1884, in *Elk v. Wilkins*, the Court held that

> Indians born within the territorial limits of the United States, members of, and owing immediate allegiance to, one of the Indian tribes (an alien, though dependent, power), although in a geographical sense born in the United States, are no more "born in the United States and subject to the jurisdiction thereof," within the meaning of the first section of the Fourteenth Amendment, than the children of subjects of any foreign government born within the domain of that government, or the children born within the United States, of ambassadors or other public ministers of foreign nations.

In 1915, in *Heim v. McCall*, the Supreme Court properly upheld New York's authority to distinguish between citizens and non-citizens and thereby show preference to citizens in hiring for public transit projects. In describing the State of New York as "a recognized unit and those who are not citizens of it are not members of it," the Court ruled that New York "could prefer its own citizens to aliens without incurring the condemnation of the National or the state constitution."

In 1927, in *Ohio ex rel. Clarke v. Deckebach*, the Supreme Court unanimously rejected the equal protection argument and upheld a Cincinnati ordinance requiring that licenses to operate pool halls be issued only to U.S. citizens.

In 1942, in *In re Thenault*, a federal court in the District of Columbia re-confirmed the conditions of citizenship:

"Of course, the mere physical fact of birth in the country does not make these children citizens of the United States, inasmuch as they were at that time children of a duly accredited diplomatic representative of a foreign state. This is fundamental law and within the recognized exception not only to the Constitutional provision relative to citizenship, Amendment Article 14, Section 1, but to the law of England and France and to our own law, from the very first settlement of the Colonies."

TAMPERING WITH NATIONAL SECURITY

Since the years of the Warren Court, the Supreme Court has obscured the fundamental constitutional definition of citizenship without dealing with it directly. The justices have toyed with their own notions of citizenship instead of sticking with the Constitution as written, and this has even interfered with our national security.

Yaser Esam Hamdi was captured in Afghanistan as an enemy combatant during our military operation there. When interviewed by a U.S. interrogation team, he identified himself as a Saudi citizen who had been born in the United States. But after being detained as an enemy combatant, he argued that he was a U.S. citizen because of his birth in Baton Rouge, Louisiana, to Saudi Arabian parents. His father, Esam Fouad Hamdi, joined the lawsuit from his country of Saudi Arabia.

There is no evidence that Hamdi ever consented to be subject to the jurisdiction of the United States, or sought to settle in the United States, or renounced his Saudi Arabian citizenship. All evidence is that he retained allegiance to Saudi Arabia.

The short answer to Hamdi's legal claim should have been that he was not an American citizen. But litigation about his rights unfortunately assumed that he was a U.S. citizen and was therefore entitled to the rights and privileges of that status. Without addressing the citizenship issue, the Supreme Court ultimately held in *Hamdi v. Rumsfeld* (2004) that Hamdi could contest his status as an enemy combatant. That forced the Bush Administration to agree to release Hamdi and deport him to Saudi Arabia in exchange for his dropping his claim to U.S. citizenship.

PREVARICATING ABOUT CITIZENSHIP

To become a naturalized U.S. citizen, it is necessary to take this solemn oath:

> I hereby declare, on oath, that I absolutely and entirely renounce and abjure all allegiance and fidelity to any foreign prince, potentate, state, or sovereignty, of whom or which I have heretofore been a subject or citizen; that I will support and defend the Constitution and laws of the United States of America against all enemies, foreign and domestic; that I will bear true faith and allegiance to the same; that I will bear arms on behalf of the United States when required by the law; that I will perform noncombatant service in the Armed Forces of the United States when required by the law; that I will perform work of national impor-

tance under civilian direction when required by the law; and that I take this obligation freely without any mental reservation or purpose of evasion; so help me God.

There is no ambiguity about this oath. To become a U.S. citizen, immigrants are required by our law not only to swear allegiance to the United States, but to absolutely renounce any and all allegiance to the nation from which they came. This oath makes clear that there can never be any divided loyalty or dual citizenship with an immigrant's native country. But again, Supreme Court justices who believe that they can legislate according to their notions of what public policy should be continued their interference in congressional jurisdiction over immigration by encouraging the mischievous notion of dual citizenship.

The U.S. Constitution, Article 1, Section 8 gives the power over naturalization law solely to Congress, not to the Court. Using its constitutional authority, Congress passed a law providing that "A person who is a national of the United States, whether by birth or naturalization, shall lose his nationality by: . . . (e) Voting in a political election in a foreign state or participating in an election or plebiscite to determine the sovereignty over foreign territory."

In a 5 to 4 vote, the Warren Court overturned this law in *Afroyim v. Rusk* (1967). The case involved a Jewish immigrant from Poland who became a U.S. citizen in 1926 and, like other naturalized citizens, took an oath renouncing his former citizenship. But in 1950 he went to Israel and voted there. The law expressly required forfeiture of citizenship for voting in a foreign election. Yet contrary to the plain words of the statute, the Court held that he did not lose his U.S. citizenship by voting in a foreign country.

Actually, Afroyim did not betray his oath because he did not vote in his native country. But unfortunately, this case has been used to promote dual citizenship by those who encourage divided loyalties among immigrants. The oath every new citizen must take should prevent naturalized U.S. citizens from voting in their native country.

Our country is now confronted with the problem that some immigrants have falsely been led to believe that they are or can be dual citizens, and Mexico is aggressively promoting the notion that Mexicans in the United States can vote in both countries. This dangerous notion would dilute our national identity and culture.

Under the U.S. Constitution, all questions of citizenship and naturalization should be made by Congress, not by supremacist judges.

— 10 —

Judges Interfere with Elections

FOR THE FIRST 174 YEARS after our Constitution was adopted, the reapportionment of state legislatures was considered a "political question" to be resolved by the legislative branch. "Courts ought not to enter this political thicket," the Supreme Court ruled in *Colegrove v. Green* (1946).

Then suddenly, in *Baker v. Carr* (1962), Justice William J. Brennan led the judicial supremacists into the thicket. Asserting the "responsibility of this Court as ultimate interpreter of the Constitution," he ruled that courts could redraw the boundaries of legislative districts. Justice Frankfurter, in dissent, joined by Justice Harlan, wrote that the *Baker v. Carr* decision was ". . . a massive repudiation of the experience of our whole past in asserting destructively novel judicial power. . . ."

Reapportionment was another new area where the judicial supremacists of the Warren Court seized legislative powers. The next step after *Baker* was Chief Justice Earl Warren's majority opinion in *Reynolds v. Sims* (1964). The Supreme Court ruled that population (one-man-one-vote) must be the primary consideration in apportionment plans for both houses of state legislatures. This forbade state legislatures from imitating the pattern of Congress, where one house is apportioned by population and the other by geography.

Further enunciating notions of judicial exclusiveness, Chief Justice Warren wrote in *Powell v. McCormack* (1969), "It is the responsibility of this court to act as the ultimate interpreter of the Constitution."

On the contrary, the U.S. Constitution does not make the Supreme Court "the ultimate interpreter of the Constitution." Such language originated with the judicial supremacists. Justices Warren and Brennan were leaders in the revolution that was taking place, case by case, to dismantle the separation of powers and replace it with judicial supremacy.

The Supreme Court's disdain for the right of the people to govern ourselves was pointed out by Justice Clarence Thomas in his brilliant dissent in *U.S. Term Limits v. Thornton* (1995):

> It is ironic that the Court bases today's decision on the right of the people to "choose whom they please to govern them." Under our Constitution, there is only one State whose people have the right to "choose whom they please" to represent Arkansas in Congress. The Court holds, however, that neither the

elected legislature of that State nor the people themselves (acting by ballot initiative) may prescribe any qualifications for those representatives. The majority therefore defends the right of the people of Arkansas to "choose whom they please to govern them" by invalidating a provision that won nearly 60% of the votes cast in a direct election and that carried every congressional district in the State.

BUSH V. GORE

The Bush-Gore election in 2000 is a case in which *state* court judicial supremacists caused unprecedented problems. The Florida ballots had been counted and recounted according to pre-election procedures. All ballot procedures had been approved by both major parties before the election, and Florida was about to certify the election in an orderly way. Al Gore was free to present evidence of fraud or other misconduct, but he had no such evidence and lost his challenge in the trial court.

Then the judicial supremacists on the Florida supreme court threw the election into chaos. They seized on Gore's argument that a different recount method might have yielded a different outcome and ordered a peculiar recount invented by the judges in order to maximize Al Gore's chances.

The Florida supreme court supremacists, in their extraordinary conceit, operated on the premise that because they were high-ranking judges, they could devise and require a recount scheme superior to the one prescribed by pre-election rules. That premise is nonsensical and un-democratic. It is absolutely essential to democratic elections to count the votes according to the rules agreed to *before* the election begins. Any deviation from the procedure agreed upon in advance makes the election less fair.

During the Supreme Court oral argument on *Bush v. Gore*, Justice Sandra Day O'Connor enunciated the best rule about what standard to apply in ballot recounts: "Why isn't the standard the one that voters are instructed to follow, for goodness' sakes? I mean, it couldn't be clearer."

Yes, the ballots should be counted in accord with the instructions provided to the voters before they vote.

The wild activism of the Florida court cried out to be stopped by someone. Fortunately, the U.S. Supreme Court put an end to the crazy post-election recount scheme in-vented by the Florida judicial supremacists.

Unfortunately, the Supreme Court failed to identify *state* court judicial supremacy as the cause of the post-election turmoil in Florida. Probably because too many Supreme Court justices are *federal* judicial supremacists, they didn't want to criticize *state* judicial supremacists. The majority opinion held only that a *judicially ordered recount* must satisfy minimal equal protection standards.

The Supreme Court decision in *Bush v. Gore* was widely criticized on federalism grounds by those who thought that the Supreme Court should have deferred to the Florida state judicial supremacists. But the Supreme Court effectively and properly deferred to Florida's legislative and executive branches, while halting the Florida judiciary's interference in the election. Justices Souter and Breyer agreed that the

Florida supreme court was interfering with the election in an unconstitutional manner, but they still wanted to use federal judicial supremacy to order their own peculiar recount schemes.

The Supreme Court annoyed many commentators who believe in judicial supremacy by saying that the *Bush v. Gore* ruling applies only to the "present circumstances." But of course *all* rulings should apply only to the case before the court. Courts are not supposed to concoct laws or rules to apply to people who are not parties to the case. As the Kennedy-Rehnquist-O'Connor-Scalia opinion stated in *Missouri v. Jenkins*, it would be "a blatant denial of due process" to apply its decision to "persons who have had no presence or representation in the suit."

But the judicial supremacists have become so accustomed to believing that Supreme Court decisions are the law of the land—instead of merely a decision on the controversy before the court—that it caused much comment when the justices restricted *Bush v. Gore* to that particular case.

THE CALIFORNIA RECALL

The California constitution has a provision for recalling a governor so he can be replaced without waiting for the next election. A populist movement in 2003 gathered the necessary petitions to recall Governor Gray Davis, and a recall election was scheduled.

With the election already underway and absentee ballots being collected, the Ninth Circuit U.S. Court of Appeals ruled 3 to 0 that the election must be postponed.

Many concluded that the judges were trying to help the Democrats, but the announced reason was that there was a likelihood that the ACLU could prove in a trial that new touch-screen computerized ballots would be more accurate than the system California had used for decades.

This decision was in the face of overwhelming evidence from academics and voter registrars that an abrupt switch to new voting technology would create its own problems and errors among voters and poll personnel. If the punch-card ballot were really illegal as the court maintained, then how could Governor Davis's original election be valid, since punch cards were used then?

The relative merits of punch-card and touch-screen ballots are not the issue. Such controversies are routinely resolved in our political system without any help from judges. The threat to self-government comes from judges who interfere with an ongoing election. The California judicial supremacists said they had to suspend the election in order for the United States to set a good example for other countries. The court said in *Southwest Voter Registration Education Project. v. Shelley* (2003): "... this is a critical time in our nation's history when we are attempting to persuade the people of other nations of the value of free and open elections. Thus, we are especially mindful of the need to demonstrate our commitment to elections held fairly, free of chaos . . . ."

Did those judges really think that the California recall election would be so chaotic that it would set a bad example for Iraq and Afghanistan? If anything, the Ninth Circuit showed us that judicial supremacists could derail an election at the last minute and create real chaos. No democratic country should ever permit judges to postpone or cancel an election. It is essential that elections proceed as scheduled.

The trial judge had found nothing objectionable about the California recall election. The only evidence cited by the three Ninth Circuit judges was that the ACLU wanted to cancel the election; that the Secretary of State had agreed to phase out punch cards; and that a study showed that touch-screens were superior to punch cards. But the study was funded by a major provider of touch-screen voting machines.

To try to justify an order to switch to a new system, the judges used some meaningless buzzwords to suggest that a perfectly good election procedure needed a high-tech replacement: ". . . the fundamental right to have votes counted in the special recall election is infringed because the pre-scored punch-card voting systems used in some California counties are intractably afflicted with technologic dyscalculia." (Judicial supremacists, elitists that they are, love to lace their opinions with words the voters don't understand.)

As it turned out, the Ninth Circuit judicial supremacists lost their nerve, and the full court let the election proceed as scheduled. The voters elected Arnold Schwarzenegger in a fair election with ordinary ballots. California counties then spent millions of dollars on computerized touch-screen election equipment, but controversies remain. On April 30, 2004, the California secretary of state banned the use of fourteen thousand touch-screen machines because of security and reliability concerns, and "decertified" an additional twenty-eight thousand until their security could be upgraded.

The court's analysis of voting systems was naive and technically flawed, as well as legally and politically abominable. It is scary to think how close we came to letting judges sabotage the most important California election in years, and there is no indication that the judges have retreated from their supremacist attitudes.

SHENANIGANS IN NEW JERSEY

The liberals in politics, media, and the judiciary have popularized the notion that an election loser can use the courts to change the rules that were in place before the election. This is a very bad idea; not even banana republics let judges interfere with elections.

In the 2002 New Jersey Democratic primary for the U.S. Senate, the incumbent Senator Robert Torricelli easily won renomination. He then dropped dramatically in the polls following corruption charges and announced his intention to withdraw. But the general election had already begun; ballots had been printed, overseas military ballots had been mailed, some servicemen had already voted, and the legal deadline for substituting another candidate had passed.

New Jersey law clearly states that a name can be substituted on the ballot "in the event of a vacancy, howsoever caused, among candidates nominated at primaries, which vacancy shall occur not later than the fifty-first day before the general election." When Torricelli announced his intention to withdraw, it was only thirty-six days before the election.

So the Democrats asked the New Jersey supreme court to rewrite the law, and the New Jersey judicial supremacists changed the rules.

The problem with the court's decision is that no change in the rules during or after an election can ever be fair. The only way to hold an honest election is to have an agreed-on procedure in advance and follow pre-election rules, whether or not one side later objects, and even if hindsight can invent a better system. If judges are allowed to manipulate elections by changing the rules in the middle of or after the election, then we can expect crooked elections.

GIVING THE FRANCHISE TO FELONS

The nation's four million convicted felons could be enough to swing future elections. Surveys show that the big majority would vote Democratic if they could, so felons are a voting bloc the Democrats are itching to acquire.

In the 2000 election, George W. Bush carried Florida by 537 votes. The Associated Press reported afterwards that as many as five thousand felons may have voted illegally, nearly 75 percent of whom were registered Democrats. In the 2004 gubernatorial election in Washington State, the Democrat was elected by a margin of 129 votes, but the Democrats later admitted that at least seven hundred felons voted illegally.

The laws of forty-eight states place restrictions on the ability of convicted felons to vote. State laws vary widely in these restrictions. State laws may distinguish between those who are now behind bars and those who have been released, or whether they are repeat offenders, or whether they are violent or nonviolent offenders, or whether they are parolees or probationers.

Allowing felons to vote is highly unpopular with the American people, but the laws are amended from time to time. Since 1996, nine states have repealed a few of their voting barriers for convicted felons, while three states made their laws tougher. These changes don't appear to have anything to do with partisanship or geography. The states easing their bans were Alabama, Maryland, Virginia, Connecticut, Delaware, Nevada, New Mexico, Texas, and Wyoming, while the states that toughened their policies were Massachusetts (by constitutional amendment), Utah and Kansas.

The Democrats haven't a chance for wholesale repeal of these laws. So the Democrats are doing what liberals always do: line up the American Civil Liberties Union and other left-wing lawyers and then seek out activist judges to issue decisions which elected legislators will not make. A massive campaign is now underway to overturn state laws that bar or restrict felons from voting. The Democrats are also trying to get the courts to rewrite the Voting Rights Act to make it applicable to felons.

To try to give convicted felons the franchise, the Democrats are playing the race card, asserting that state laws have a "disparate impact" on blacks and Hispanics and therefore violate equal-protection guarantees. The laws, of course, are color-blind, and, furthermore, it is no more discriminatory to deny felons their franchise than to deny them certain categories of employment, child custody, or gun ownership.

In *Johnson v. [Jeb] Bush*, a panel of the Eleventh Circuit U.S. Court of Appeals by 2 to 1 in 2003 reversed a district court ruling and ordered a trial on the race allegations in Florida even though the plaintiffs presented no evidence of any racial animus. The decision was written by one of Clinton's most controversial nominees, Judge Rosemary Barkett. The dissenting opinion pointed out that the Fourteenth Amendment, Section 2, "explicitly allows states to disenfranchise convicted felons." Furthermore, the dissent explained, in the time period when Florida adopted the rule against voting by felons, no "disparate impact" on minorities existed, so there could not have been any bias in the adoption of the rule. In April 2005, the Eleventh Circuit *en banc* reversed, and the U.S. Supreme Court, on November 14, 2005, refused to hear the case.

In *Farrakhan v. Locke* (2003), a U.S. District Court in Spokane dismissed a case brought by prison inmates, but the liberal Ninth Circuit sent the case back for a trial. In *Muntaqim v. Coombe*, the Second Circuit expressed uncertainty and confusion about the felons issue and is now reconsidering this case *en banc*. The plaintiff, Jalil Munatqim, was convicted of the ambush murder of two New York police officers.

New Jersey allows felons to vote after they complete their incarceration, parole, or probation, but that's not enough to please the Democrats. Ten ex-convicts (including a convicted killer) are suing to void the state law, backed by the Constitutional Litigation Clinic at Rutgers Law School, the ACLU, the New Jersey State NAACP, and the Latino Leadership Alliance of New Jersey.

Activist judges who like to cite foreign law and create new "human rights" based on "emerging awareness" may soon be invoking Britain's October 2005 decision to grant the franchise to its 77,000 prisoners. Britain kowtowed to the European Court of Human Rights in Strasbourg, which ruled that the "right to free elections" applies to prisoners. The case was won by a prisoner who killed his landlady with an axe.

The U.S. Constitution reserves the matter of voting regulations to state legislatures and specifically authorizes the disenfranchisement of felons. We should not permit supremacist judges to rewrite these laws.

- 11 -

Judges Take Over
Parents' Rights

AMILY COURT JUDGES may be the most powerful judges in the American judicial system. While they are the lowest in the judicial hierarchy, they have become the most activist and unaccountable of all courts because of the tremendous number of families and amounts of money under their control.

The U.S. Census Bureau reported that, in 2002, 13.4 million parents had custody of 21.5 million children under age twenty-one whose other parent lived somewhere else. Along with the 13.4 million "other parents," these Census Bureau figures imply that judges have control over the private living arrangements and income of 48.3 million Americans—one sixth of our population.

The Census Bureau also reported that, in 2002, $40 billion in transfer payments were made between households. That money is under the direction and control of family court judges.

These shocking statistics show that family courts are now an arm of government that routinely exercises virtually unlimited power to dictate the private lives and income of millions of American citizens who have committed no actionable offense. The reason these figures are so extraordinary is that family courts exercise the same power to dictate the private lives and income of parents who are self-supporting, law-abiding, and responsible in the care of their children, as family courts exercise over parents who are none of those things.

Major social trends of the past three decades, including no-fault divorce, illegitimate births, the feminist movement, the redefinition of domestic violence, and aggressive enforcement of household-support laws, have vastly increased the number of Americans who come into family courts. Decisions of family court judges are seldom reported in law books and seldom appealed or reviewed. Not only do few people have the funds to finance an appeal, but since decisions are a matter of judicial discretion, the chances of overturning a family court judge are close to zero unless gross judicial abuse can be proved.

Divorcing parties who separate amicably and reach a private final agreement to divide their property may not realize the power of the family court. Decisions about child custody and household support are never final and are always subject to attack by either parent. One parent can challenge a private custody agreement at any time for any reason. The family court has the power to ignore private agreements about child custody, even if in writing and signed, and order new custody and support terms on the theory that new circumstances require the court to reevaluate its prior decision. Family court judges amassed these powers by co-opting and changing the definition of a time-honored concept: "the best interest of the child."

The original concept of the best interest of the child comes from English common law as compiled by William Blackstone in 1765, who said that parents are presumed to act in their own children's best interest. Courts honored parents' rights by recognizing a legal presumption that the best interest of the child is whatever a fit parent says it is, and that a court should not second-guess a parent or substitute its own opinion.

About thirty years ago, as states revised their family-law statutes, the concept of best interest of the child became disconnected from parents' decisions. Family courts got the idea that they have discretion to make independent decisions about what is in a child's best interest, especially for children of divorced or unmarried parents, even though little or no objective standards are set forth in statutes.

The concept that persons other than parents are better able to decide what is the best interest of a child is illustrated by the slogan "it takes a village to raise a child."

The notion that the "village" should make childrearing decisions rather than parents is manifested in the way the public schools have taken over many responsibilities traditionally in the domain of parents, such as providing meals, healthcare, and pre-kindergarten services. Public schools notoriously assert their right to override parental decisions about the assignment of books that parents find immoral or profane, the use of privacy-invading questionnaires, teaching about sex and evolution, the provision of contraceptives and abortion referrals, the use of school counselors, and demands that children be injected with vaccines or put on psychotropic drugs.

The growing power of the public schools to override parents' rights is evident in the 2005 Ninth Circuit outrage, *Fields v. Palmdale School District.* The opinion, written by Jimmy Carter–appointed Judge Stephen Reinhardt (who had earlier declared that one atheist could silence all school-children from reciting the Pledge of Allegiance), was joined by two other judges, one appointed by Bill Clinton and the other by Lyndon B. Johnson. These three supremacists ruled, based on "our evolving understanding of the nature of our Constitution," that parents' fundamental right to control the upbringing of their children "does not extend beyond the threshold of the school door," and that a public school has the right to provide its students with "whatever information it wishes to provide, sexual or otherwise."

Best interest of the child is totally subjective; it's a matter of individual opinion. Parents make hundreds of different decisions and should have the right to make their own decisions, even if they contravene custom. Whether the decision is big (such as living in an urban or rural neighbor-hood) or small (such as playing baseball or soccer), there is no objective way to say which is better.

Since judges are supposed to base their decisions on evidence presented in open court, and there is no societal consensus about the best way to raise a child, they have demanded the testimony of expert witnesses. A big industry has grown up of psychologists, psychiatrists, social workers, custody evaluators, and counselors who are eager to give their opinions. Having opinions produced by so-called experts with degrees or professional certification is a way to make a subjective and arbitrary judgment appear objective. With the ever-increasing volume of family cases coming through the courts, judges began rubber-stamping the opinions of these court-appointed experts.

The use of so-called experts by family courts has become standard procedure. Divorced parents are routinely "sentenced" to submit to psychological evaluations (often by persons who have no experience with raising a child), and to parenting classes designed to re-educate the parent according to the instructors' biases (which may include hostility to spanking, the military, religion, and homeschooling).

Court-appointed evaluators purport to judge the parents' parenting capacity and determine custody, but no scientific basis exists for their methodologies, for the tests they use, or for the recommendations they make. There is no agreement among professionals on how to conduct a proper examination, what standards to use if any, or what should go into an assessment. The evaluators' reports are not scientific findings but expressions of personal preference. The use of people other than parents to determine the best interest of a child cannot be justified by science, law, morality, or common sense. Even if there were a way to define "best interest," it would lead to all sorts of undesirable consequences. Should we take children away from poor parents and give them to richer parents? Of course not.

When a judge makes a decision based on the best interest of the child, there is no way to determine whether the decision is correct. A family court judge has tremendous power to do whatever he wants in determining the lifestyle of American families, the authority parents have over their own children, and the time each parent is permitted to spend with his or her own children.

The decisions of family court judges are effectively final because a judge's decision can be reversed only for abuse of discretion, and it's not clear what, if anything, could constitute abuse of such unlimited discretion.

When one parent files for divorce, that parent sur-renders both parents' authority to decide "best interest" to the judge, who then divides the parental custody time into shares that are usually vastly unequal. The parent with the larger share is labeled the custodial parent, and the parent with the smaller share is called the non-custodial parent.

Census Bureau figures show that 85 percent of custodial parents are mothers. The father, who is typically designated the non-custodial parent, is customarily allowed "visitation" with his child every other weekend. The father's presence in the child's life is thus lowered to 20 percent, more or less.

Even more significantly, as a non-custodial parent, his authority as a father is reduced to zero, and his right to make childrearing decisions is eliminated. The father's value to the family is reduced to providing a paycheck and being an occasional visitor. No statute requires this unequal division of time or parental authority: it's all done by judicial discre-tion. Why a parent's rights should be denied or diminished after divorce has never been explained; after all, it is the husband and wife who are divorcing, not the children.

When divorced parents disagree, as for example, about which religion the child will be taught, judges must leave this important decision to the parents to work out themselves no matter how much conflict may ensue. Disagreements about numerous other matters, great and small, involved in the raising and education of a child inevitably arise, but a judge should not be allowed to take over any fit parent's power to participate in decisions—or bargain with an ex-spouse about them. Transferring child-raising decisions to a judge should not be the solution.

Every successful civilization has placed the shared responsibility for rearing the next generation on married parents. Replacing that proven practice with the notion that "a village" should raise children according to an assortment of outside opinions of what is in a child's "best interest" is a radical departure from the traditional rule that married parents should possess shared responsibility for raising their own children. This change in social policy has not proved successful anywhere, and history offers numerous examples of unsuccessful alternate patterns.

We have already witnessed the unhappy consequences of our government's liberal welfare policy (starting with Lyndon Johnson's Great Society in the 1960s) which, by channeling money through the mother, thereby relieving the father of duties and decision-making power, has changed the welfare class into a matriarchal society. The tragic results are obvious. Most of our social problems are caused by the 40 percent of our nation's children who grow up in homes without their own father: drug abuse, illicit sexual activity, unwed pregnancies, youth suicide, high school dropouts, joblessness, runaways, and crime.

The best interest of the child rule, which typically eliminates both the authority and the presence of the father, is now doing to the middle class what the mistaken welfare policy has already done to the welfare class.

Other constitutional rights can also disappear in family court. If a man is accused (but not tried or convicted) of being an imperfect father (or of not conforming to "village" opinions about child-raising), he loses constitutional rights as well as his children. Restraining orders (orders of protection) are widely used by women in divorce cases as a weapon to gain total custody of the children. The *Illinois Bar Journal* called restraining orders part of "the gamesmanship of divorce."

Divorce should not deprive parents of the fundamental right to rear their children. Children should not be deprived of their father and of father-parenting, which (contrary to feminist ideology) is different from mother-parenting and just as essential to the child's well-being.

No one, not even a judge, should have the awesome power to take away the fundamental right and authority of a parent over his own minor child in the absence of a criminal conviction or life-endangering circumstance. No one, not even a judge, should have the awesome power to deprive a child of his or her father by reducing the father's role in the family to providing a paycheck and a few days of "visitation." That level of power produces supremacist judges—those who think they are supreme enough to dictate the lives of individual Americans.

— I2 —

Judges Impose Taxes

Aprime example of judicial supremacist mischief was the federal district court's imposition of increased property taxes in Kansas City to pay for the world's most extravagant public school facilities. In *Jenkins v. Missouri* (1985), the district court simply ignored the principle that the taxing power is a purely legislative function, definitely not one for the courts. James Madison wrote in *Federalist 48*: "The legislative branch alone has access to the pockets of the people."

This highly controversial case bounced around in federal courts for years. When it finally reached the Supreme Court in *Missouri v. Jenkins* (1990), Justice Anthony Kennedy's opinion, joined by Justices Rehnquist, O'Connor and Scalia, concurred in part with the majority decision to uphold the court-ordered tax, but included a scathing indictment of judicial supremacists:

> The Court . . . goes further, much further, to embrace
> by broad dictum an expansion of power in the federal

judiciary beyond all precedent. Today's casual embrace of taxation imposed by the unelected, life-tenured Federal Judiciary disregards fundamental precepts for the democratic control of public institutions. . . .

The judicial taxation approved by the Eighth Circuit is also without parallel. . . . The description of the judicial power nowhere includes the word "tax," or anything that resembles it. This reflects the Framers' understanding that taxation is not a proper area for judicial involvement. . . . A judicial taxation order is but an attempt to exercise a power that always has been thought legislative in nature. . . .

The judiciary is not free to exercise all federal power; it may exercise only the judicial power. . . . The power to impose burdens and raise money is the highest attribute of sovereignty, and is exercised, first, to raise money for public purposes only; and, second, by the power of legislative authority only. It is a power that has not been extended to the judiciary. . . . The power of taxation is one that the federal judiciary does not possess.

We often hear it said that Supreme Court decisions are the law of the land, not merely the law of the case. That heresy has crept into conventional wisdom over the last fifty years. This concurring opinion by four justices, warning that *Missouri v. Jenkins* "cannot be seen . . . as precedent for the future," shows that, every now and then, the justices recognize that their decisions should apply only to the parties involved in the case before them.

The four justices' opinion explained the sequence of how such overreaching decisions evolve. "Judicial taxation" was first endorsed in dicta in Eighth Circuit cases in which taxation orders were in fact disapproved. Then the activist judges on the Eighth Circuit built on the dicta and, for the first time in history, ordered judicial "taxation to fund a remedial decree."

Again and again in this concurring opinion, Justices Kennedy, Rehnquist, O'Connor, and Scalia reminded the Supreme Court majority that they have no constitutional authority to tax the American people. Continuing to point out the overreaching of *Missouri v. Jenkins*, this opinion states that imposing a tax wasn't even necessary to achieve the goal of providing equal protection to minority schoolchildren.

The four justices' opinion concludes by saying that *Missouri v. Jenkins* "is a stark illustration of the ever-present question whether ends justify means." The judicial supremacists opted to pursue the end of integrating Kansas City schools not only by violating the Constitution but by ordering unprecedented taxes to pay for an incredibly costly capital improvement plan that included

> high schools in which every classroom will have air conditioning, an alarm system, and 15 microcomputers; a 2,000-square-foot planetarium; greenhouses and vivariums; a 25-acre farm with an air-conditioned meeting room for 104 people; a Model United Nations wired for language translation; broadcast capable radio and television studios with an editing and animation

lab; a temperature controlled art gallery; movie editing and screening rooms; a 3,500-square-foot dust-free diesel mechanics room; 1,875-square-foot elementary school animals rooms for use in a Zoo Project; swimming pools; and numerous other facilities.

All that tax-funded extravagance turned out to be a colossal waste. Not only did the end not justify the means, but the desired end wasn't even achieved. Two decades and billions of dollars later, the Kansas City schools are just as segregated as ever and test scores are just as low.

BULLYING NEVADA'S LEGISLATURE

Some *state* court judges have also swallowed the heresy that judges can impose taxes.

Nevada voters approved a constitutional amendment by a wide margin in 1996 to require a two-thirds vote in the state legislature for new or increased taxes. In 2003, the Nevada legislature was deadlocked in a budget dispute and had to either raise taxes or cut spending in order to balance the budget. The governor wanted a tax increase, so he persuaded the Nevada supreme court to issue an advisory ruling that the legislature could pass a tax increase with a simple majority (ignoring the two-thirds constitutional requirement).

The legislature then did precisely that, allowing itself to be bullied by the judicial supremacists on the state court. The Speaker of the Assembly declared the tax increase passed, based on the court's opinion in *Guinn v. Legislature of the State* (2003).

The Nevada court rationalized its opinion by saying that the constitutional mandate to fund education was more important than the procedural limit on tax increases. But Nevada did not have to raise taxes in order to fund education. It could have just funded education at previous levels.

Taxation and funding decisions should always belong to the people and their elected representatives, not to judges. In order to avert a constitutional crisis, the legislature later repassed the tax increase with a two-thirds vote.

The *Las Vegas Review* later reported that the Nevada supreme court decision was an advance deal between the governor and the court, that the governor spoke with the supreme court judges at the beginning of the budget battle and received assurances from them that the court would approve his proposed tax hike.

SUPREMACISTS HIDE BEHIND CHILDREN

If any issues should be solely legislative prerogatives, they are raising taxes and spending the taxpayers' money. But in recent years Congress and state legislatures have been, for the most part, wisely unwilling to raise taxes. So what are tax-and-spend liberals to do?

Run to supremacist judges, of course. State judges have responded enthusiastically to lawsuits that invite them to showcase their powers, and schools offer an inviting target.

Courts not only are issuing orders to pour more taxpayers' money into public schools but are micromanaging
schools, telling them how much money to spend and on
what, right down to making decisions about computers
and textbooks.

The famous Kansas City case (*Missouri v. Jenkins*), in
which the Supreme Court swallowed hard but nevertheless
approved a court-ordered tax increase, gave a big boost to
school finance litigation, and it has since become a billion-
dollar business. Schools are desirable plaintiffs: the lawsuits
are "for the children."

In the 1970s, activist judges were ordering schools to
spend more money to achieve racial balance. But forced
busing turned out to be expensive, disruptive, and unpro-
ductive.

When judges and lawyers began to see that desegregation was an academic failure and minorities began filing
suits to return to neighborhood schools, the rationale for
school litigation changed to "equity." Dozens of suits were
filed in the 1980s under equal protection clauses in state
constitutions to get activist judges to order state tax levies
to equalize spending on schools in rich and poor districts.

"Equity" has been a spectacular failure, too. It did little
or nothing to improve test scores. Spending disparities
between districts were narrowed in some cases, but Education Trust, a Washington-based research group, found that
in half the states the funding gap between rich and poor
districts actually widened.

In the 1990s, the lawyers changed their takeover rationale again. They abandoned the argument of "equity" and

sought out subjective words in state constitutions such as "thorough and efficient," "sound basic," "adequate," "quality," or "suitable." "Adequate" became one of the most popular words. These words gave great power to the courts—only a judge could be wise enough to determine exactly how many millions of tax dollars are "adequate."

The New York Court of Appeals, after ten years of litigation, ruled that the taxpayers must spend 43 percent more money to provide schoolchildren a "sound, basic education." A court-appointed panel ordered New York City to spend an additional $5.6 billion, plus $9.2 billion on new classrooms, laboratories, libraries, and other facilities, making tax increases inevitable.

In Montana, the state supreme court decided in 2004 that the school financing system was fatally flawed and ordered the legislature to appropriate more money to give children "a basic system of free, quality public elementary and secondary schools."

Kentucky is still in court sixteen years after activist judges first intervened to tell the state how to run its schools. A 1981 lawsuit filed against New Jersey was decided four years later, but has since returned to court nine times.

Kansas became ground zero in the battle to transfer tax-and-spend powers from state legislatures to state courts. The Kansas supreme court in *Montoy v. Kansas* (2005) ordered the legislature to put nearly a billion dollars more money into the public schools, even though Kansas already spends nearly $10,000 per pupil, pays teachers more than most Kansas workers, and graduates students who score well in national tests.

The judges seized on the word "suitable" in the state constitution and ruled that its definition means a specific amount of money knowable only to judges. The court gave the legislature a deadline and threatened to close all the state's schools unless the legislature obeyed the court order by a date certain.

Some valiant Kansas legislators tried to retain the legislature's authority over spending. Senator Kay O'Connor said, "Folks, we have a constitutional crisis. If we bow down to their orders, where does it end?" But the constitutionalists were outvoted by those who chose to accept the court's arrogant ruling as the law of the land. There may have been another motive. The capitol corridors were filled with gambling lobbyists who whispered that the legislature could avoid a tax increase if it would instead vote to bring casinos into the state.

Lawsuits are pending in twenty-four states asking judges to order the state legislature to pour lots more money into the public schools which, obviously, will require tax increases. Activist judges have accepted these adequacy arguments in most major school finance decisions since 1989.

The tremendous amounts of money and the financial burden that these state court decisions impose on the taxpayers are mind-boggling. No end is in sight because of the ingenious ways that liberals try to get courts to order the spending of taxpayers' money. University of Virginia law professor James E. Ryan, for example, argues that "a very strong legal case, based on education clauses within every state constitution, can be made on behalf of a state constitutional right to preschool."

This is all taking place under the radar of public notice because most of the news coverage is local and the local politicians are afraid to challenge the public school establishment and the unions.

The case of *Flores v. Arizona*, which has been pending in federal court in Tucson since 1992, exemplifies many of the worst supremacist notions described in this book. A Carter-appointed judge ruled in 2000 that federal law requires Arizona "to take appropriate action to overcome language barriers that impede equal participation" by the estimated 160,000 children of illegal aliens (euphemistically called "English Language Learners") in Arizona's public schools.

When that judge retired, the *Flores* case was handed off to a Clinton-appointed judge, who decided in 2005 that "appropriate action" means spending much more money and imposed fines of $500,000 a day, escalating in stages to $2 million a day, for every day that the legislature failed to appropriate the money the judge demanded. With millions of dollars in fines accumulating since January 25, 2006, the judge has effectively taken the power of taxing and spending away from the state legislature.

~ 13 ~

How Judicial Supremacy Began

F EDERAL JUDGES AND LAW PROFESSORS all say that the most important legal case in American history is the U.S. Supreme Court case of *Marbury v. Madison* (1803). They assert that this case established the principle of judicial review and made it central to our legal and political system.

Marbury v. Madison was, in fact, a narrowly decided case. It became significant because of the way that later judges have used it. The facts were simple, but the opinion is convoluted. Thomas Jefferson called it "merely an *obiter* dissertation of the Chief Justice."

In the last days of his administration, President John Adams appointed William Marbury to the minor office of justice of the peace, but the formal commission was never delivered to him. After Thomas Jefferson became president, Marbury sued, asking the court to issue a writ of mandamus ordering Secretary of State James Madison to deliver Marbury's commission. Chief Justice John Marshall ruled that the congressional law authorizing the Supreme Court to issue writs of mandamus to public officers was unconstitutional, so the Court could not issue the writ and Marbury didn't get the job.

One sentence in John Marshall's decision articulated the power of judicial review and the Court's authority to declare laws unconstitutional: "It is emphatically the province and duty of the judicial department to say what the law is." That key sentence has been used to promote judicial review, a concept that is not in the Constitution. Since the Warren Court, it has also been used to promote judicial supremacy.

But there is a huge difference between a judiciary that says what the law *is*, and a judiciary that insists what *it* says *is* the law. The former is the rule of law; the latter is judicial tyranny. There is no quarrel with judicial review in the way it was carried out in *Marbury*. If a law is clearly unconstitutional, the courts *should not* enforce it. Judicial review is a long, long way from the judicial supremacy we suffer today.

Marbury v. Madison was actually a model of judicial restraint, not an activist decision. Marshall narrowly construed the Court's own powers and refused to accept what he thought was an unconstitutional grant of power by Congress to the courts. Marshall then refused to interfere with the presidential appointments.

The two sentences that immediately follow the famous line quoted above show that Marshall simply meant that the courts should apply the law in particular cases and resolve any conflict between two laws as necessary to decide the case. Later in *Marbury*, Marshall wrote that the Constitution is "a rule for the government of courts, as well as the legislature" and that "courts, as well as other departments, are bound by that instrument." *Marbury v. Madison*, therefore, did not give us judicial supremacy. *Marbury* did no damage to our separation of powers.

It was fifty-four years before the Supreme Court declared another federal law unconstitutional. During all those years, our nation's leaders understood the proper role of the judiciary, and they never espoused any theories of judicial exclusiveness. For example, President Andrew Jackson's veto of the bill to recharter the Bank of the United States (July 10, 1832) stated: "The Congress, the Executive, and the Court must each for itself be guided by its own opinion of the Constitution. Each public officer who takes an oath to support the Constitution swears that he will support it as he understands it, and not as it is understood by others."

Jackson's often-quoted remark in regard to another controversy, "John Marshall gave his opinion, now let him enforce it," may be apocryphal. But if he didn't say it, he could have said it because presidents and justices in those years knew and accepted their proper role under the separation of powers, recognizing that we should not permit one court opinion to decide major policy questions.

EMBARRASSMENT FOR SUPREMACISTS

The judicial supremacists like to cite *Marbury v. Madison* because it is just too embarrassing to cite the case that really started judicial supremacy: *Dred Scott v. Sanford* (1857), the first case in which the Supreme Court tried to expand its power over other branches of government. It was for many reasons one of the most disastrous decisions in history.

Dred Scott was a black slave who traveled to free territories and then sued for his freedom. Instead of simply deciding the controversy, the Supreme Court handed down an aggressively activist, judicially supremacist, pro-slavery decision. It dismissed Dred Scott's complaint, saying that he didn't even have the right to be a plaintiff in a lawsuit: blacks "had no rights which the white man was bound to respect," and even the free blacks in the Northern states didn't have the right to be citizens. The Court declared unconstitutional the federal law, passed in 1820 as part of the Missouri Compromise, forbidding slavery in most of the Western territories. It was only the second federal law in history declared unconstitutional.

The Constitution limits the jurisdiction of the federal courts to "cases and controversies." Federal courts are not supposed to give advisory opinions about issues that are not before them as a case or controversy. *Dred Scott* is a good example of the Court trying to decide issues that were not necessary to its decision, and the Court ended up causing gross injustices.

Abraham Lincoln refused to accept that the Supreme Court could set public policy, and he endured much criticism for attacking the *Dred Scott* decision. But Lincoln was absolutely correct in identifying not only the intrinsic wrongness of the decision, but also its terrible consequences in upsetting our form of government.

In his First Inaugural Address (March 4, 1861), Lincoln admitted that the Supreme Court decision was personally binding on plaintiff Dred Scott, but Lincoln expressed the hope that its "evil effect" would be "limited to that particular case, with the chance that it may be overruled and never become a precedent for other cases." In other words, Lincoln accepted judicial review as binding in the case, but he rejected judicial supremacy—the notion that the Supreme Court was supreme in creating new laws for the nation—because that would abolish self-government and submit us to the rule of judges. Lincoln identified the evil of judicial supremacy: "If the policy of the government upon vital questions affecting the whole people is to be irrevocably fixed by decisions of the Supreme Court, the instant they are made in ordinary litigation between parties in personal actions, the people will have ceased to be their own rulers, having to that extent practically resigned their government into the hands of that eminent tribunal."

Precisely. Lincoln agreed that the Supreme Court could decide the fate of Dred Scott. But Lincoln rejected the notion that an "eminent tribunal" should be allowed to make public policy. That would mean submitting to the rule of judicial supremacists rather than to the Constitution and the rule of law.

Lincoln defied the *Dred Scott* opinion by issuing passports to blacks and otherwise treating them as citizens, and he signed legislation to place limits on slavery in the Western territories. The *Dred Scott* decision exacerbated the conflict over efforts to restrict slavery and pushed our country toward a terrible war to correct the injustice wrought by the power-grabbing Supreme Court.

Anyone who thinks that we need judicial supremacy to protect the rights of minorities must accept that judicial supremacists gave us the injustice of the *Dred Scott* decision. Anyone who thinks we need judicial supremacists to protect civil rights should remember George Washington's warning that we should permit the Constitution to be amended only in the way that the Constitution provides: "Let there be no change by usurpation; for though this, in one instance, may be the instrument of good, it is the customary weapon by which free governments are destroyed."

— 14 —

How Judicial Supremacy Grew

A HUNDRED YEARS WENT BY after *Dred Scott v. Sanford.* Then came the gigantic grab for judicial supremacy led by Chief Justice Earl Warren, a politician who had no previous judicial experience. His ideology was so mixed that both Republican and Democratic parties nominated him for governor of California. He was appointed to the Supreme Court as the political payoff for delivering the sixty-eight votes of the California delegation to help Dwight Eisenhower defeat Robert A. Taft at the 1952 Republican National Convention. Ike later admitted that he regretted the appointment.

As California's attorney general, Warren had presided over the infamous internment of Japanese-Americans during World War II. After he assumed the title of Chief Justice, he seemed to believe he could use Supreme Court decisions to write his own political views into law. In a 2005 speech at Vanderbilt University, Justice Scalia blamed Chief Justice Earl Warren for increasing the political role of the

Supreme Court, saying that Warren had been "a governor, a policy-maker, who approached the law with that frame of mind."

No sooner was Warren confirmed as Chief Justice than he began to assert judicial supremacy, overturning established laws about criminal procedures, prayer in schools, internal security, obscenity, and legislative reapportionment. In those days, not only the public but the legal community objected vigorously to the high-handed, wrong-headed decisions of what became known as the Warren Court.

Even the associate justices on the Warren Court realized that Supreme Court decisions were going so far afield from proper judicial authority that they were in fact amending the Constitution. Justice Hugo Black dissenting, joined by Justice Tom Clark, wrote that the New York criminal law knocked out in the *Jackson v. Denno* decision (1964) ". . . should not be held invalid by the Court because of a belief that the Court can improve on the Constitution."

Justice John Harlan, in dissent, wrote that the Court's action in *Reynolds v. Sims* (1964) ". . . amounts to nothing less than an exercise of the amending power by this Court. . . . For when, in the name of constitutional interpretation, the Court *adds* something to the Constitution that was deliberately excluded from it, the Court in reality substitutes its view of what should be so for the amending process."

ASSAULT ON INTERNAL SECURITY

In 1957 the American Bar Association (ABA) Committee on Communist Tactics, Strategy and Objectives, chaired by Herbert R. O'Conor, a former Democratic U.S. Senator from Maryland, presented the annual ABA Convention delegates with a stinging criticism of fifteen decisions in which the Warren Court had ruled in favor of Communists and against U.S. internal security. At that time, Soviet Communism was the greatest threat to American security. Communist spies had infiltrated high levels of our government and stolen our atomic bomb secrets.

All fifteen decisions were reversals of lower court decisions. Most of them voided laws or procedures which the ABA Committee, the Congress, and the American people believed were necessary to protect our national security. The ABA report pointed out that "the repeal or the weakening of these anti-Communist laws and committees is in the forefront of the program of the Communist Party of the United States." (See Appendix for the list of cases.)

Pennsylvania v. Steve Nelson, one of those fifteen cases, was an example of the new Warren Court doctrine of making law for the whole country instead of just deciding only the case before the Court. The Supreme Court not only held it was unlawful for Pennsylvania to prosecute a Pennsylvania Communist Party leader under the Pennsylvania Sedition Act, but indicated that the anti-sedition laws of forty-two other states (which were not parties to the case) likewise could not be enforced.

The ABA report emphasized that many of the cases represented a direct attack on the authority of Congress to conduct investigations in order to do its job of legislating. Prior to the Warren Court, the Supreme Court had always refused to interfere with the investigative function of congressional committees. A unanimous Court had ruled in *McGrain v. Daugherty* (1927): "The power to legislate carries with it by necessary implication ample authority to obtain information needed in the rightful exercise of that power, and to employ compulsory process for the purpose."

But the Warren Court demonstrated its disrespect for Congress's constitutional authority to conduct investigations by drastically clipping Congress's investigative and legislative powers, as well as powers of the executive branch and of federal and state law enforcement agencies to protect our national security.

The media treated the ABA report as big news. Headlines in New York newspapers proclaimed: "Bar Association Told High Court Weakens Security Against Reds" and "Warren Court Kicked in Teeth." *U.S. News & World Report* published the text of the ABA report.

U.S. News & World Report also published an analysis by Senator James O. Eastland of the way the Warren Court ran roughshod over laws and procedures for the benefit of the Communists. This included a tally on whether the individual justices voted to uphold the position advocated by the Communists or not. Hugo Black voted to uphold the Communist position in every one of seventy-one decisions. William O. Douglas voted for the Communists in sixty-six cases, against them in three. Felix Frankfurter's score was fifty-six to sixteen. Earl Warren's score was thiry-six to three. William Brennan's score was eighteen to two. Senator Eastland showed that "the Court has been expanding its

usurpation of the legislative field and purporting to make
new law of general application which will be favorable to
the Communist position."

In the early days of the new era of judicial supremacy,
Congress and the media had the courage to speak out
against Supreme Court arrogance. Close observers clearly
understood that the Warren Court was making dramatic
departures from previous Courts, that it was boldly seizing legislative functions, and that Congress had a duty to
halt the Court's assault on other branches of government.
On August 7, 1957, the Senate Subcommittee on Internal
Security held a hearing on the "Limitation of Appellate
Jurisdiction of the United States Supreme Court" at which
Senator William E. Jenner testified: "There was a time
when the Supreme Court conceived its function to be the
interpretation of the law. For some time now, the Supreme
Court has been making law—substituting its judgment
for the judgment of the legislative branch. . . . We witness
today the spectacle of a Court constantly changing the law,
and even changing the meaning of the Constitution, in an
apparent determination to make the law of the land what
the Court thinks it should be."

After spelling out how the Supreme Court had indulged
in unprecedented activism in the areas of criminal procedure
and property law, Jenner addressed himself particularly to
the decisions that dismantled U.S. internal security:

> What shall we say of this parade of decisions that came
> down from our highest bench on Red Monday after
> Red Monday? The Senate was wrong. The House of

Representatives was wrong. The Secretary of State was wrong. The Department of Justice was wrong. The State legislatures were wrong. The State courts were wrong. The prosecutors, both Federal and State, were wrong. The juries were wrong. The Federal Bureau of Investigation was wrong. The Loyalty Review Board was wrong. The New York Board of Education was wrong. The California bar examiners were wrong. The California Committee on Un-American Activities was wrong. The Ohio Committee on Un-American Activities was wrong. Everybody was wrong except the attorneys for the Communist conspiracy and the majority of the United States Supreme Court. . . .

That is why we in Congress must fulfill our plain duty and act immediately in the way the Constitution empowers us to act, to repair as much of the damage as we can and prevent even worse damage in the future.

But Congress failed to do its plain duty. Congress did not act to protect the authority of the legislative branch against judicial tyranny. So the judicial supremacists keep seizing more and more power over the other branches of government in many areas of law, and Americans are still suffering the consequences.

MISREADING MARBURY V. MADISON

The case that gave legal life to the false but now widely held concept of judicial supremacy is *Cooper v. Aaron* (1958). It wasn't the decision itself, but the extra unnecessary language in the opinion that facilitated the justices' grab for power.

The facts in this case were fairly simple. Desegregation of the public schools in Arkansas in 1958 was highly controversial. The Little Rock school board sought a postponement of the desegregation program and won approval in the U.S. District Court. That decision was reversed by the U.S. Court of Appeals, and the Supreme Court affirmed the appellate court's decision to go forward with immediate desegregation. The Court could have ended its opinion right there. Indeed, the Court admitted this, stating: "What has been said, in the light of the facts developed, is enough to dispose of the case."

But instead of confining itself to implementing the timetable for desegregation ordered by the Court of Appeals, the Supreme Court immediately added a "However" and proceeded to use the desegregation issue to elevate the federal judiciary to the most powerful branch of government. Claiming that it was quoting "some basic constitutional propositions which are settled doctrine," *Cooper v. Aaron* asserted that John Marshall's famous line from *Marbury v. Madison* (1803) had "declared the basic principle that the federal judiciary is supreme in the exposition of the law of the Constitution, and that principle has ever since been respected by this Court and the Country as a permanent and indispensable feature of our constitutional system. It follows that the interpretation of the Fourteenth Amendment enunciated by this Court in the *Brown* case is the supreme law of the land. . . ."

None of this was "settled doctrine." *Cooper v. Aaron* was not merely a restatement of *Marbury v. Madison. Marbury v. Madison* did not claim that "the federal judiciary is supreme." The notion was not a "basic principle." No such supremacy theory had previously been recognized as an "indispensable feature of our constitutional system." No one before had ever asserted that a Supreme Court decision is "the supreme law of the land." The Constitution clearly defines the supreme law, and the judiciary is not part of the definition.

When judges ramble on in their opinions with discussions that are unnecessary to the decision, their extra words are called "dicta." Dicta have been with us from the beginning of the federal courts, but in the 1950s the Warren Court began pretending that dicta were part of the decisions. These gratuitous words have now become so common in court opinions that many people don't realize that they are beyond the scope of judicial authority.

Many mistakenly believe that *Brown v. Board of Education* was the landmark case that changed everything, but it wasn't. *Brown* simply reversed the Court's 1896 pro-segregation decision of *Plessy v. Ferguson.* The vast expansion of judicial authority by the Warren Court was not caused by *Brown v. Board of Education.*

Cooper v. Aaron was the case that grabbed judicial exclusiveness and supremacy over the other branches of government. And it was all so unnecessary to accomplish the goal of school desegregation. *Cooper* was the work of a petty politician, Earl Warren, reaching for power to which he was not entitled. Then, having gotten by with *Cooper v. Aaron*'s grab for power by intimidating anyone who might challenge it, the judicial supremacists extended their new authority into other areas.

More and more frequently, we began to hear the refrain that the U.S. Constitution is whatever the Supreme Court says it is. Supreme Court Justice Stephen Breyer, in his new book *Active Liberty*, openly attacks strict construction and "textualism." He urges us to accept the notion that U.S. constitutional law is whatever a majority of the Supreme Court justices decide, based on their own notions of "democracy" and "active liberty." His book illustrates the difference between a justice appointed by Bill Clinton (Breyer) and a justice appointed by George W. Bush (Samuel Alito), who said in his confirmation hearings: "I think we should look to the text of the Constitution, and we should look to the meaning that someone would have taken from the text of the Constitution at the time of its adoption."

The concept of judicial supremacy did not originate with the Constitution, and it did not come from *Marbury v. Madison*. It is an outrageous assertion of judicial exclusiveness that dates from unprecedented overreaching by the Warren Court in the 1950s and 1960s. Yet it has now become so ingrained in our legal culture that many people wonder how our society could function without it. What is needed today is for judges to return to their traditional respect for the Constitution and its separation of powers into three branches.

~ 15 ~

How to Stop
Judicial Supremacists

OUR TASK IS TO EXPUNGE the un-American notion
of judicial supremacy by using the checks and
balances built into our great United States Constitution. We must stop the judicial supremacists who have
been systematically dismantling the architecture of our
unique, three-branch constitutional republic and replacing
it with an Imperial Judiciary. Since the legal community
has a vested interest in the status quo, this task must be un-
dertaken by grassroots Americans. We must raise a mighty
demand that Congress do its duty.

Out-of-control federal and state judges who believe in
and advocate judicial supremacy over the other branches of
government are trying to write new laws and to invalidate
laws and practices that have been part of American life for
centuries. If the American people don't stand up for the
Pledge of Allegiance, the Ten Commandments, and the
sanctity of marriage, what do we stand for?

The American people must *not* acquiesce in illicit grabs for power by federal and state judges who censor and over-turn our precious laws and traditions. We must reject the notion that judges' orders in particular cases are the law of the land that we must all obey. Congress, the executive branch, and the American people must use every peaceful weapon at our disposal.

We must press forward with the task of confirming nominees who respect the Constitution. We must also deal with the problem of the activist judges who are undermining the Constitution under the shield of life tenure. Hundreds of judicial supremacists with lifetime appointments are on the federal bench today and could be there for decades more.

We must also address the problem of judges who be-come activists and supremacists after they don their black robes and become heady with their new powers.

President George W. Bush's 2004 State of the Union Address, which targeted "activist judges" as the enemy of traditional values and urged us to use "the constitutional process" to remedy their mischief, was spoken in the context of the threat to the traditional definition of marriage. His remarks are equally applicable to other institutions that are precious to Americans, including the Pledge of Allegiance and the Ten Commandments.

Here are ten steps to terminate the rule of judges and restore constitutional self-government.

I

REFORM SENATE RULES

The Senate must reform its rules so liberals are not able to defeat constitutionalist nominees by preventing the Senate from voting them up or down. We should not eliminate the filibuster; we should make it a fair and workable process.

The current Senate Rule XXII requires sixty senators (three-fifths of the entire U.S. Senate) to close debate and proceed to a vote. That means the Republicans must have sixty votes on the floor to break a filibuster, but the Democrats can keep the filibuster going with only a single Senator on the floor (to make objections). By this method, the Democratic minority in the Senate won sixteen cloture votes and successfully blocked some of President Bush's best nominees to the U.S. Courts of Appeals.

The Senate should adopt a new rule permitting three-fifths of Senators *present* to close a debate. That would give the majority a fair chance to confirm the president's nominees by requiring the obstructionist minority to actually show up and debate.

We expect Republican senators to do their duty by confirming constitutionalist judges after ascertaining that they believe in upholding the U.S. Constitution as it was written and do not subscribe to the notion that it is a living and evolving document. We hope Justice Samuel Alito will be faithful to his statement to the Senate Judiciary Committee in 1990 that judges should not "import a judge's own view of the law into the law that should be applied to the case."

II

LEGISLATE EXCEPTIONS TO COURT JURISDICTION

Congress has the duty to curb the power of the judicial supremacists. We don't trust the federal courts or the Supreme Court to tamper with the definition of marriage by applying supremacist notions of "emerging awareness" or "evolving paradigm." We don't trust the courts to tamper with our right to acknowledge God, whether in the Pledge of Allegiance, the Ten Commandments, our national motto, or voluntary prayer. Therefore, Congress should remove power from all federal courts to impose the rule of judges over our rights of self-government.

Our great Constitution has within it the checks and balances we need to deal with the problem of judicial supremacy. This includes the ability of Congress to limit the jurisdiction (judicial power) of all federal courts.

Article 1, Section 8 of the Constitution states: "The Congress shall have power . . . to constitute tribunals inferior to the Supreme Court." Article III, Section 1 states: "The judicial power of the United States, shall be vested in one Supreme Court, and in such inferior courts as the Congress may from time to time ordain and establish." These two sections mean that all federal courts except the Supreme Court were created by Congress, which defined their powers and prescribed what kind of cases they can hear. Whatever Congress created it can abolish, limit, or regulate.

Article III, Section 2 states: "The Supreme Court shall have appellate jurisdiction, both as to law and fact, with such exceptions, and under such regulations as the Congress shall make." This section means that Congress can make "exceptions" to the types of cases that the Supreme Court can decide. This is the most important way that Congress can bring an end to the reign of judicial supremacy.

There is nothing new or wrong about Congress telling the federal courts what cases they can and cannot hear. Limiting court jurisdiction is a tool the liberals have used many times. In 2002, Congress passed a law (at Senator Tom Daschle's urging) to prohibit all federal courts from hearing cases about brush clearing in South Dakota. Surely other issues are as important as brush fires in South Dakota.

The Record of Congressional Action

A long historical record conclusively proves that Congress has the power to regulate and limit court jurisdiction, that Congress has used this power repeatedly, and that the courts have accepted it.

In *Turner v. Bank of North America* (1799), Justice Chase commented: "The notion has frequently been entertained, that the federal courts derive their judicial power immediately from the Constitution; but the political truth is, that the disposal of the judicial power (except in a few specified instances) belongs to Congress. If Congress has given the power to this Court, we possess it, not otherwise: and if Congress has not given the power to us, or to any other Court, it still remains at the legislative disposal."

Even Chief Justice John Marshall, the judicial supremacists' hero, made similar assertions. For example, in *Ex parte Bollman* (1807), Marshall said that "courts which are created by written law, and whose jurisdiction is defined by written law, cannot transcend that jurisdiction."

The early decisions of the Supreme Court were sprinkled with the assumption that the power of Congress to create inferior federal courts necessarily implied, as stated in *U.S. v. Hudson & Goodwin* (1812), "the power to limit jurisdiction of those Courts to particular objects." The Court stated, "All other Courts [except the Supreme Court] created by the general Government possess no jurisdiction but what is given them by the power that creates them."

The Supreme Court held unanimously in *Sheldon v. Sill* (1850) that because the Constitution did not create inferior federal courts but rather authorized Congress to create them, Congress was also empowered to define their jurisdiction and to withhold jurisdiction of any of the enumerated cases and controversies. This case has been cited and reaffirmed numerous times. It was applied in the Voting Rights Act of 1965, in which Congress required covered states that wished to be relieved of coverage to bring their actions in the District Court of the District of Columbia.

The Supreme Court broadly upheld Congress's constitutional power to define the limitations of the Supreme Court "with such Exceptions, and under such Regulations as the Congress shall make" in *Ex parte McCardle* (1869). Congress had enacted a provision repealing the act that authorized the appeal McCardle had taken. Although the Court had already heard argument on the merits, it dismissed the case for want of jurisdiction. "We are not at liberty to inquire into the motives of the legislature. We can only examine into its power under the Constitution; and the power to make exceptions to the appellate jurisdiction of this court is given by express words."

McCardle grew out of the stresses of Reconstruction, but the principle there applied has been affirmed and applied in later cases. For example, in 1948 Justice Frankfurter in *National Mutual Insurance Co. v. Tidewater Transfer Co.* (dissenting) commented: "Congress need not give this Court any appellate power; it may withdraw appellate jurisdiction once conferred and it may do so even while a case is *sub judice* [already before the court]."

In *The Francis Wright* (1882), the Court said:

> While the appellate power of this court under the Constitution extends to all cases within the judicial power of the United States, actual jurisdiction under the power is confined within such limits as Congress sees fit to prescribe. . . . What those powers shall be, and to what extent they shall be exercised, are, and always have been, proper subjects of legislative control. . . . Not only may whole classes of cases be kept out of the jurisdiction altogether, but particular classes of questions may be subjected to re-examination and review, while others are not.

Numerous restrictions on the exercise of appellate jurisdiction have been upheld. For example, Congress for a hundred years did not allow a right of appeal to the Supreme Court in criminal cases except upon a certification of divided circuit courts.

In the 1930s, liberals in Congress thought the federal courts were too pro-business to fairly handle cases involving labor strikes. In 1932 Congress passed the Norris-La-Guardia Act removing jurisdiction in this field from the federal courts, and the Supreme Court had no difficulty in upholding it in *Lauf v. E. G. Shinner & Co.* (1938). The Supreme Court declared, "There can be no question of the power of Congress thus to define and limit the jurisdiction of the inferior courts of the United States."

Liberals followed the same procedure when they passed the Hiram Johnson Acts in order to remove jurisdiction from the federal courts over public utility rates and state tax rates. These laws worked well and no one has suggested they be repealed.

Another celebrated example was the Emergency Price Control Act of 1942, in which Congress removed from federal courts the jurisdiction to consider the validity of any price-control regulation. In the test case upholding this law, *Lockerty v. Phillips* (1943), the Supreme Court held that Congress has the power of "withholding jurisdiction from them [the federal courts] in the exact degrees and character which to Congress may seem proper for the public good."

After the Supreme Court ruled in *Tennessee Coal v. Muscoda* (1944) that employers had to pay retroactive wages for coal miners' underground travel to and from their work station, Congress passed the Portal-to-Portal Act of 1947 prohibiting any court from enforcing such liability.

Even one of the leading judicial supremacists, Justice William Brennan, conceded Congress's constitutional power to limit the jurisdiction of the federal courts. In 1982 he wrote for the Court in *Northern Pipeline Construction Co. v. Marathon Pipe Line Co.*: "Of course, virtually all matters that might be heard in Art. III courts could also be left by Congress to state courts . . . [and] the principle of separation of powers is not threatened by leaving the adjudication of federal disputes to such judges."

In 1999 the Court upheld Congress's power to restrict the jurisdiction of the federal courts to interfere in certain immigration disputes (*Reno v. American-Arab Anti-Discrimination Committee*). In 2003 a federal judge upheld a 1996 law signed by President Clinton that gave exclusive authority to the U.S. attorney general to deport certain illegal aliens and specified that federal courts have no jurisdiction to review such removal orders (*Hatami v. Ridge*).

Another statute that prohibits judicial review is the Medicare law, on which nearly everyone over age sixty-five relies for health care. Congress mandated that "there shall be no administrative or judicial review" of administrative decisions about many aspects of the Medicare payment system. When someone sued in federal court anyway, the court dismissed the lawsuit based on this prohibition of judicial review. (*American Society of Dermatology v. Shalala*, 1996).

In 2005, Congress passed the Protection of Lawful Commerce in Arms Act which forbids both federal and state courts from entertaining suits against gun manufacturers for the misuse of their lawfully sold firearms, canceled all such suits currently in the courts, and gives similar immunity to private individuals who are legal gun owners. This act protects gun manufacturers and individuals from having to pay the penalty for the crimes of others. While this law was passed under Congress's Commerce Clause power rather than Article III, the effect is very much the same: Congress has prohibited the courts from hearing certain kinds of lawsuits.

Justices Recognize Congress's Authority

Supreme Court justices know perfectly well that Congress has Article III power to limit their jurisdiction. When Chief Justice Rehnquist issued his last annual report, he spent several pages discussing criticism of the courts and arguing against Congress ever using its power to impeach judges. He then included this sentence: "There were several bills introduced in the last Congress that would limit the jurisdiction of the federal courts to decide constitutional challenges to certain kinds of government action."

Rehnquist made no additional comment or explanation. He didn't say such action would be undeserved or unconstitutional or unwise or out of the mainstream. He just left that sentence for us to construe either as an invitation to congressional action or as a warning to his associates.

When Chief Justice John Roberts was special assistant to the attorney general during the Reagan Administration, he wrote a twenty-seven page document defending the constitutional power of Congress to limit federal court jurisdiction. To prove that Supreme Court justices recognize this power over the courts, he pointed out that former Supreme Court Justice Owen Roberts had proposed an "amendment of the Constitution to remove Congress' exceptions power," which was actually passed by the Senate in 1953 but then tabled by the House. John Roberts concluded that Congress's constitutional authority to make exceptions to federal court jurisdiction is so clear that only a new constitutional amendment could deny it.

Keep Judges' Hands Off DOMA

The Defense of Marriage Act (DOMA), overwhelmingly passed by Congress in 1996, defines marriage for federal purposes as "a legal union between one man and one woman as husband and wife," and assures that states do not have to recognize same-sex marriage licenses issued by other states. Congress must defend this good and popular law.

It is completely constitutional for Congress to take away from all federal courts the power to declare federal and state DOMAs unconstitutional—and it's Congress's constitutional duty to protect the American people from judicial supremacists who might commit such an outrage. The House of Representatives did pass a bill to accomplish this in the fall of 2004, but the Senate took no action. Since lawyers are predicting it is only a matter of time until federal courts knock out DOMA, Congress would be derelict in its duty if it doesn't protect DOMA from out-of-control federal judges.

Congress should also withdraw jurisdiction from federal courts to hear any case claiming that state DOMAs violate the U.S. Constitution. Such a law would protect us from the ruling of the federal judge who knocked out Nebraska's state constitutional amendment that was passed by 70 percent of the voters.

Legislation to limit federal court jurisdiction will not stop Massachusetts from issuing same-sex marriage licenses.

But it would mean that the federal government would not have to recognize those licenses and that the federal courts could not be used to force other states to recognize them.

—

The executive branch also has the responsibility to defend marriage by using DOMA. The President should do his constitutional duty to "take care that the laws be faithfully executed."

The General Accounting Office compiled a fifty-eight-page list of 1,049 federal rights and responsibilities that are contingent on DOMA's definition of marriage. The GAO report states that the man-woman marital relationship is "integral" to the Social Security system and "pervasive" to our system of taxation. The widespread social and familial consequences of DOMA also impact on adoption, child custody, veterans benefits, and the tax-free inheritance of a spouse's estate.

The Internal Revenue Code has provided since 1948 that "a husband and wife may make a single return jointly of income taxes." If the highest court of a state declares that marriage is no longer a union of "husband" and "wife," then whatever unions are performed in that state should not be recognized as a marriage by federal law and should not be entitled to file a joint federal income tax return.

Gay advocates want same-sex couples to claim the 1,049 benefits of marriage under federal law, but what should happen instead is that, once a state's definition of marriage no longer means husband and wife, then no one married in that state (including opposite-sex couples) should be recognized as married by federal law. Couples that seek traditional marriages recognized by the federal government for income tax purposes might consider traveling to another state that performs only marriages that are legitimate under federal law.

The President should order the bureaucracy to establish procedures to handle the paperwork. Taxpayers are quite used to having to provide the Social Security number of their children to prove their existence in order to claim income tax exemptions. The Internal Revenue Service should prepare income tax forms that require joint returns to show the date and place of marriage, enabling it to identify and reject unions from states, cities, counties, and foreign countries whose local marriage laws do not comply with the federal definition of marriage.

The President should instruct all federal agencies to prepare for energetic compliance with the more than a thousand federal regulations impacted by DOMA.

Keep Judges' Hands Off Acknowledgment of God

Congress should pass a law to clarify that the federal courts, including the Supreme Court, do *not* have jurisdiction over whether an acknowledgment of God by public officials violates the Establishment Clause of the First Amendment. Nothing in the Constitution confers on the federal courts, including the Supreme Court, the final and exclusive authority to decide how the other branches, or how each governmental entity of the fifty states, may acknowledge God. Under the constitutional doctrine of separation of powers, each branch of the federal government has the authority to determine how it will acknowledge God.

This remedy is needed because dozens of cases have been filed all over the country asking federal judges to declare the recitation in public schools of the Pledge of Allegiance unconstitutional because it includes the words "under God," or demanding that the display of the Ten Commandments in public buildings be held unconstitutional.

The federal courts should have no authority to hear such cases or to render such a decision. These lawsuits are initiated under the pretense that any mention of God violates the First Amendment, which states: "Congress shall make no law respecting an establishment of religion, or prohibiting the free exercise thereof . . . ." The acknowledgment of God in the Pledge of Allegiance and the Ten Commandments is not an "establishment of religion." The Constitution delegates "all legislative powers" to the Congress (none to the courts), and Congress has never passed a law banning the acknowledgment of God.

So how could a handful of activist judges in the last couple of years presume to ban the acknowledgment of God from documents, monuments, songs, expressions and practices that have been part of our culture throughout our history? The answer is that Congress and the American people have been letting them get by with this unconstitutional grab for power.

The federal courts should have no jurisdiction to consider cases involving the acknowledgment of God. Congress should forbid federal courts from censoring public acknowledgments of God, adding this issue to other "exceptions" and "regulations" to federal court jurisdiction.

That is the way the framers of our Constitution intended that Congress would, as Alexander Hamilton wrote in *Federalist 78*, keep the judiciary as the "least powerful" branch of government and see to it that judges "should be bound down by strict rules and precedents, which serve to define and point out their duty."

III

STOP FOREIGN INTERFERENCE

Congress should prohibit federal courts from relying on foreign laws, administrative rules, or court decisions. Americans have been shocked to learn that six U.S. Supreme Court justices cited foreign sources, even though it is self-evident that U.S. judges should be bound by the U.S. Constitution and U.S. laws, *not* foreign ones.

One of the justifications for the American Revolution listed in the Declaration of Independence was that King George III had "combined with others to subject us to a jurisdiction foreign to our Constitution, and unacknowledged by our laws." It is unacceptable that Supreme Court justices have gone on record as saying that U.S. court decisions should be influenced by foreign sources.

In a speech to the U.S. Judicial Conference on March 16, 2004, House Judiciary Committee Chairman F. James Sensenbrenner Jr. admonished the justices that deference to foreign sources is out of order:

Article VI of the Constitution unambiguously states that the Constitution and federal statutes are the supreme law of the land. America's sovereignty may be imperiled by a jurisprudence predicated upon laws and judicial decisions unfounded in our Constitution and unincorporated by the Congress. Inappropriate judicial adherence to foreign laws or legal tribunals threatens American sovereignty, unsettles the separation of powers carefully crafted by our Founders, and threatens to undermine the legitimacy of the American judicial process.

IV

STOP JUDICIAL TAXATION

Congress should prohibit the federal courts from ordering any government entity at any level to raise taxes or spend taxpayers' money under any circumstance. One of the Constitution's clearest directives is "All Bills for raising Revenue shall originate in the House of Representatives."

State court judges must also be required to recognize that under the separation of powers, raising taxes and appropriating money are exclusively legislative functions.

V

CONGRESS SHOULD USE ITS MONEY POWER

Congress should pass legislation to prohibit the spending of federal money to enforce obnoxious decisions handed down by judicial supremacists. The House of Representatives did exactly this when it passed two amendments in 2003 sponsored by Rep. John Hostettler (R-IN). One amendment, which passed 307 to 119, would have prohibited spending federal money to enforce the Ninth Circuit's anti-Pledge of Allegiance decision, and the second, adopted 260 to 161, would have done likewise for the Eleventh Circuit ruling that the Ten Commandments may not be posted in the Alabama state courthouse. On June 15, 2005, the House passed another Hostettler bill to prohibit tax funds from being used to enforce the ruling of a district court in Indiana that had ordered the removal of a Ten Commandments monument in Gibson County, Indiana. Unfortunately, the Senate failed to act on those bills.

Since Congress controls appropriations, there are many ways that Congress can rein in the courts, such as refusing to allow any federal funds to be used when local governments misuse the power of eminent domain for purposes other than constitutionally valid "public use." Congress can use its appropriations power to negate any court opinion such as *Fields v. Palmdale School District* (2005) which purports to terminate parents' rights over sex education in public schools. Congress should make compliance with the law about parents' rights a condition of federal funding to schools just like other civil rights requirements.

Although the Constitution forbids Congress from reducing the salaries of federal judges "during their continuance in office," Congress could cut the administrative budget of the judiciary to limit, for example, their foreign junkets where they pick up so many bad ideas. Congress controls the money, and Congress should use its money power to limit the mischief of the judicial supremacists.

VI

END THE POWER OF A SINGLE JUDGE

Congress should take away the power of a single federal judge to issue an injunction to overturn a referendum and prevent enforcement of the voters' wishes during the years that a case winds its way through the court system. It is an offense to the rule of law that, again and again, a single federal judge has nullified an initiative passed by a majority of the voters in a statewide referendum.

A single Jimmy Carter-appointed federal judge (Mariana Pfaelzer) nullified California's Proposition 187, which would have prohibited giving taxpayer benefits to illegal aliens. Proposition 187, which passed in 1994 receiving five million votes, was nullified by only one federal judge and kept permanently inoperative (*League of United Latin American Citizens v. Wilson*).

A single federal judge nullified Proposition 209, the California Civil Rights Initiative to end state racial preferences, which overwhelmingly passed in 1996. It is nonsense to call this measure unconstitutional when its text reads as if it were copied from the 1964 Civil Rights Act. Judge Thelton Henderson, the Carter appointee and former ACLU board member and civil rights litigator who rendered this decision, not only used his judicial power to overturn the wishes of the majority of Californians, but in a highly suspect procedure, grabbed jurisdiction over this case from another judge to whom it had been assigned. Fortunately, the Ninth Circuit ruled that Proposition 209 is constitutional (*Coalition for Economic Equity v. Wilson*) and declared, "A system which permits one judge to block with the stroke of a pen what 4,736,180 state residents voted to enact as law tests the integrity of our constitutional democracy."

Indeed it does. We wish the Ninth Circuit would always remember that principle.

In a statewide referendum in 1991, the voters in the state of Washington reaffirmed a state statute that prohibited anyone from "knowingly causing or aiding other persons in ending their lives." In *Compassion in Dying v. Washington* (1996), one federal district court judge (Barbara J. Rothstein) declared unconstitutional the people's vote against physician-assisted suicide. The full Ninth Circuit U.S. Court of Appeals, *en banc*, agreed, tried to invent a new constitutional right to assisted suicide, and smeared those who oppose it as "cruel."

Fortunately, the Supreme Court reversed that cruel decision (*Washington v. Glucksberg*, 1997). Unfortunately, that's not the end of the story.

Five of the justices in *Glucksberg* indicated that if the facts are slightly different in a future case, they might use substantive due process to find a right to assisted suicide. In a speech on April 27, 2004, Justice Scalia speculated that the Court may soon discover a right to assisted suicide between the lines of the text of the Constitution. "We're not ready to announce that right," he said, "check back with us."

Congress should by law prevent one federal judge from overturning the vote of the people in a statewide referendum. One way to do this would be to legislate that a popular initiative passed by the voters can be struck down only by a three-judge panel.

—

Cases in which the Supreme Court was split on a decision that declared a provision of a federal or state law unconstitutional are among the most controversial and historic cases ever decided: legal tender, slaughterhouse, income tax, child labor, minimum wage, the gold clause, congressional term limits, mandatory abortion funding, partial-birth abortion, school vouchers, and racial preferences. On such great issues where our leaders and the American people have different views, does it make sense that one justice in a 5 to 4 decision should be able to void a law for the entire nation?

On the fifth anniversary of Justice Harry Blackmun's death, in March 2004, the Library of Congress made available to the public 530,000 pages of his personal papers. The documents reveal the power and influence of a single justice in legislating public policies of tremendous significance.

Blackmun's notes reveal that the Supreme Court was on the verge of rejecting by 5 to 4 the argument that prayer at public school graduations violates the First Amendment when, suddenly, Justice Anthony Kennedy changed his mind. Kennedy then wrote the 5 to 4 decision in *Lee v. Weisman* (1992) which banned graduation prayer because "peer pressure" to attend graduation might induce students to listen to a prayer they didn't like.

Lee v. Weisman became a major precedent in the cases to ban the words "under God" from the Pledge of Allegiance. Without the Kennedy switch, we probably wouldn't have to worry about the Pledge of Allegiance cases, and we might even be closer to a return to voluntary school prayer.

Why did Kennedy switch? Who influenced him at the last minute? Should such important issues of public policy be made by a single justice whose opinion shifts back and forth, and who may have been unduly influenced by pressures unknown?

Kennedy played the same role in *Planned Parenthood v. Casey*, another landmark ruling in 1992. Blackmun's notes reveal that Kennedy was ready to be part of a 5 to 4 decision overturning *Roe v. Wade*. Suddenly, Kennedy sent a handwritten note to Blackmun (the author of *Roe v. Wade*) promising "welcome news." Kennedy switched sides and joined the unexpected 5 to 4 ruling in *Planned Parenthood v. Casey* to uphold *Roe v. Wade*. Kennedy also switched from his vote upholding capital punishment for juveniles in the 5 to 4 decision in *Stanford v. Kentucky* (1989) to his vote banning juvenile capital punishment in the 5 to 4 decision in *Roper v. Simmons* (2005).

The justices' insistence on deliberating in total secrecy makes this process unaccountable to the public. It is unacceptable that one justice can willy-nilly switch sides in momentous cases for reasons unknown and thereby provide the fifth vote to bind an entire nation. It is an insult to our rights of self-government that the fickle nature of one man, combined with the utmost secrecy, leaves 290 million Americans prey to whatever happens behind the scenes.

The judicial supremacists are just as dangerous in the lower federal courts and in many state courts. The second Florida supreme court decision throwing out the 2000 presidential election count was 4 to 3, and the Massachusetts court decision in *Goodridge* legalizing same-sex marriage was also 4 to 3. As one Massachusetts legislator said, "Abraham Lincoln said government of the people, by the people, for the people, but the Massachusetts court has given us government by four people."

We must reject the notion that the Constitution is whatever the Supreme Court says it is—that, in effect, the Constitution is what one justice says it is, one justice who changes his mind overnight.

VII

REMOVAL IS AN OPTION

Congress should let it be known that it takes its impeachment power seriously and intends to use it. The Constitution's Article VI states that "all executive and judicial officers, both of the United States and of the several states, shall be bound by oath or affirmation, to support this Constitution," and Article III further specifies that all federal judges, including Supreme Court justices, "shall hold their offices during good behavior."

Making outrageous rulings that have no basis in the Constitution should be grounds for impeachment. Claiming that an Imperial Judiciary can make our laws rather than elected representatives should be grounds for impeachment. Citing foreign courts as a basis for overturning U.S. laws should be grounds for impeachment. Grounds for impeachment should also include three absurd and unconstitutional opinions issued in 2005: Judge Lawrence Karlton banned the Pledge of Allegiance, Judge Joseph Bataillon knocked out the Nebraska state constitutional amendment on marriage, and Judge Stephen Reinhardt tried to cancel all parents' rights in public schools.

Even the threat of impeachment is useful. When federal district judge Harold Baer allowed a confessed drug dealer to suppress evidence of her crime, Senate Majority Leader Bob Dole called for his impeachment and President Clinton's spokesman issued what was understood to be a veiled warning. Baer quickly reversed himself.

Impeachment should be a particularly viable remedy against judicial supremacists on state courts. The Massachusetts judges who ruled for same-sex marriage should be prime candidates for impeachment and removal.

Massachusetts even has a separate procedure to fire a sitting judge by a simple majority vote of the legislature. Article 98 of the Massachusetts Constitution provides that "the governor, with the consent of the council, may remove them [all judicial officers] upon the address of both houses of the legislature . . ." Why hasn't the Massachusetts legislature acted? It is primarily Massachusetts' duty to remedy the outrage of its out-of-control judges.

The problem of state court supremacists can also be dealt with by defeating them for reelection or retention, since they do not have lifetime appointments. The voters sent a powerful message in 1986 when California Chief Justice Rose Bird and two like-minded justices were defeated and removed for imposing their personal political views.

In 2004, Judge Gordon Maag, who had become a symbol of excessive civil litigation and the need for tort reform, was removed from the Illinois appellate court after failing to receive 60 percent of the vote in his retention election.

Illinois' unique requirement of a supermajority for judicial retention is an excellent idea which should be copied in other states.

Public indignation can sometimes achieve the same result. In 2004, a Sarasota, Florida, circuit court judge decided to retire rather than seek reelection after he was criticized on national television for allowing a criminal to remain on probation, despite violating its conditions, who was then charged with kidnapping and slaying an eleven-year-old girl.

VIII
STOP JUDICIAL MICROMANAGEMENT

Congress should prohibit federal judges from trying to micromanage public schools, prisons, or mental hospitals. The courts have no competence for these tasks, and the pretense that they do results in much mischief. For example, in *Missouri v. Jenkins*, the judicial supremacists ordered "a wholesale shift of authority over day-to-day school operations from parents, teachers, and elected officials to an unaccountable district judge whose province is law, not education." The mountain of litigation and costs that resulted from that decision achieved nothing.

Courts make no attempt to study the effects of their rulings, and sometimes the solution is worse than the problem. The Kennedy-Rehnquist-O'Connor-Scalia concurring opinion in *Missouri v. Jenkins* pointed out that the decision "demonstrated little concern for the fiscal consequences of the remedy that it helped design."

Unfortunately, judicial supremacists did not learn any lesson from *Missouri v. Jenkins*. In November 2002, the Arkansas high court ordered changes in the state's $1.8 billion public education system and set January 1, 2004, as the deadline for compliance. When the legislature failed to obey the court's orders, the Arkansas supreme court appointed its own representative to take charge of the school system.

On April 26, 2004, a Massachusetts superior court judge issued a 300-page advisory ruling, dictating the future of education in that state and giving the school system a "limited period of time" to comply. This outrage was overturned by the Massachusetts supreme court (perhaps smarting from bad publicity over its same-sex marriage decision).

On May 11, 2004, a state district judge ordered Kansas to close all its public schools until the state obeys the court's demand to change the way the taxpayers' money is spent on education.

The means by which federal district judges micromanage public agencies such as schools and prisons is called the consent decree. In a consent decree, the representatives of the parties to a lawsuit "consent" to a "decree" in which the agency is supervised by a federal court for an indefinite period of time. Some consent decrees have lasted twenty-five years or more with no end in sight—twenty-five years in which an important agency of state or local government has been taken away from legislators, voters and taxpayers, and controlled exclusively by one unelected federal district judge with life tenure.

Congress should end the racket of consent decrees by adding this provision to federal law: The equitable power of the district courts over government agencies is hereby limited to remedies that can be performed within one year. No injunction or decree or other remedy shall be entered against a governmental entity unless by its terms it can be performed within one year from date of entry.

Senator Lamar Alexander (R-TN) has introduced legislation called the Federal Consent Decree Fairness Act. The bill would make it easier for state and local governments to amend federal court consent decrees by requiring plaintiffs to justify the continued existence of consent decrees after four years have passed or six months after voters have elected a new administration.

Alexander cited examples of consent-decree abuses that this bill would remedy. In Tennessee, a federal judge ruled that the government could not scale back benefits for optional beneficiaries of the state Medicaid program in order to save health-care programs for low-income children. In New York, a thirty-year-old consent decree has forced Hispanic children into bilingual education programs over the objections of their own parents who want their children to learn English rapidly. In Los Angeles, consent decrees have forced the Metropolitan Transit Authority to spend forty-seven percent of its budget on city buses, leaving only half the budget to pay for all other Los Angeles transportation needs.

Judges have large caseloads and are constantly complaining about being overworked. The day-to-day management of schools, prisons, health care, and transit systems should not be on their agenda.

IX
CUT OFF ATTORNEY'S FEES

Congress should pass a law to prevent the collection of attorney's fees by special-interest organizations that litigate against the acknowledgment of God or marriage. It is intolerable that the ACLU and other left-wing groups are able to use these lawsuits as a source of revenue. Many of the mischievous ACLU lawsuits are actually funded by the taxpayers because a federal law awards attorney's fees if they win the case. The fees collected can be staggering.

The organizations that sued to remove the Ten Commandments from the Alabama State Judicial Building (ACLU, Southern Poverty Law Center, and Americans United for Separation of Church and State) collected $540,000 in attorney's fees and expenses in 2004 from Alabama taxpayers. It is unconscionable that the Alabama taxpayers were forced to pay for the anti-Ten Commandments lawyers.

Kentucky taxpayers handed over $121,500 to pay the ACLU for its action against the Ten Commandments display outside its state capitol, and Hamilton County, Tennessee, paid the ACLU $50,000 for the same "offense." In Georgia, the Barrow County commissioners agreed to pay the ACLU $150,000 as part of a court agreement to remove a posting of the Ten Commandments. Defending the case cost the county an additional $264,000.

The ACLU profited enormously, collecting $790,000 in legal fees plus $160,000 in court costs, as a result of its suit to deny the Boy Scouts of America the use of San Diego's

Balboa Park for a summer camp, a city facility the Scouts had used since 1915. The ACLU argued that the Boy Scouts must be designated a "religious organization" because it refuses to accept homosexual scoutmasters, and because the Scouts use an oath "to do my duty to God and my country."

Congress should end this racket. Most lawsuits do not award attorney's fees to the winner, and the law should not give a financial incentive to those suing to stop our acknowledgment of God. Federal law should never have permitted an award of attorney's fees in those cases. The attorneys who sued to remove the Ten Commandments monument in Alabama were not lawyers in private practice who risked their own time and money to help a worthy but penniless plaintiff; they were salaried lawyers employed by wealthy organizations that use such lawsuits for fundraising.

When small units of government receive a demand from the ACLU to remove their Ten Commandments monument, which may have stood in the city park for a half century without annoying anyone, many city fathers feel compelled to knuckle under because they lack the funds to fight the lawsuit. In northern Minnesota, the Duluth city council voted 5 to 4 to acquiesce in the ACLU's demand to remove a Ten Commandments monument from public property. Council members voted that way only because the city couldn't afford to pay the legal costs of defending the monument, in addition to the ACLU's fees if they lost. In May 2004 under pressure from the ACLU, the city of Redlands, California, "voluntarily" changed its forty-year-old city seal to remove a cross and replace it with a tree.

"We cannot afford to engage in a fight that we will lose," the mayor said.

There are sixteen thousand public school districts in the United States that could become targets of lawsuits to ban the Pledge of Allegiance or the Boy Scouts. No one knows how many depictions of the Ten Commandments or crosses are in courthouses or other public properties. The ACLU and other anti-God groups could look upon all of them as containing pots of gold to be captured by filing suit before a supremacist judge and then getting the judge to award generous attorney's fees.

X

THE POWER OF CONGRESSIONAL INVESTIGATIONS

The Senate and House Judiciary Committees should hold extensive hearings on various proposals to stop the usurpation of power by the federal courts. Congress's investigative function is one of its most important duties, and now is the time to use it. Many experts and scholars have proposed various remedies to curb judicial usurpation, and Congressional hearings are the proper forum to air them.

Some have proposed term limits for Supreme Court and other federal judges. That would require a constitutional amendment, since the Constitution provides that federal judges serve "during good behavior." Since 1970, justices have been staying on the Supreme Court more than ten years longer, on average, than they did in our first two centuries. Vacancies happen less often, and so nominations are more hard-fought. We passed a constitutional amendment limiting presidents to eight years, so why can a Supreme Court justice serve for thirty-six or more years?

Alternatively, Congress could pass a law requiring Supreme Court justices to move to senior status after eighteen years, as other federal judges already do. They would still draw their full salaries (as the Constitution requires) and could sit on other federal courts, but not on the Supreme Court. Or they could resign to make more money in the private sector.

Another reform proposal is to divide up the huge San Francisco-based Ninth Circuit, which now covers California and eight other states. The Ninth Circuit is the locus of many supremacist decisions, many of which have been reversed by the Supreme Court.

We must educate the public. Here is one striking example of how public discussion outside of the courtroom can correct the judges and lawyers who are teaching error.

From about 1950 to about 1990, law professors, prosecutors and judges adopted the erroneous view that the Second Amendment had nothing to do with an individual's right to own a gun. They tried to reinterpret the text of the Second Amendment, and they completely ignored its plain meaning and historical context.

Then, an assortment of gun rights advocates, working entirely outside the legal profession, actively promoted the truth about the historical meaning of the Second Amendment. At first, the legal community scoffed at these people by pretending they were ignorant "gun nuts." But eventually, the weight of logic and historical evidence became overwhelming.

The view that the Second Amendment guarantees the right of individuals to own guns has now been adopted by the U.S. Justice Department, the Fifth Circuit U.S. Court of Appeals, and a leading treatise on constitutional law. The Fifth Circuit decision, *U.S. v. Emerson* (2001), concluded that "It appears clear that 'the people,' as used in the Constitution, including the Second Amendment, refers to individual Americans."

Quoting what he called the "unanimous understanding of the Founding Fathers," Attorney General John Ashcroft stated on May 17, 2001, "In light of this vast body of evidence, I believe it is clear that the Constitution protects the private ownership of firearms for lawful purposes."

Congressional investigations into all the constitutional issues discussed in this book would take us far toward remedying the impudence of the judicial supremacists.

THE TIME FOR ACTION IS NOW

The new ruling class of judicial supremacists has effectively changed the definition of "the supreme law of the land" *from* "this Constitution, and the Laws of the United States which shall be made in Pursuance thereof" *to* whatever a federal judge decides this week. The supremacists have replaced our three equal branches of the federal government with the Imperial Judiciary.

Judges have convinced themselves that they are infallible and should have the final say over our nation's controversial political and social issues. Judges use their assumed powers to enforce their liberal agenda on us, and they preempt criticism by repeatedly proclaiming the false court-invented notions that their rulings are the law of the land and that the Constitution is whatever the Supreme Court says it is. They are locking in what Thomas Jefferson called "the despotism of an oligarchy" of judges who have become "the ultimate arbiters of all constitutional questions."

Article IV, Section 4 of the Constitution guarantees "to every State in this union a Republican Form of Government." As long as we allow judges to legislate, we do not have republican self-government. The American people and their elected representatives allowed this to happen over the last fifty years, exactly as Thomas Jefferson warned: "The germ of dissolution of our federal government is in the constitution of the federal judiciary; . . . working like gravity by night and by day, gaining a little today and little tomorrow, and advancing its noiseless step like a thief over the field of jurisdiction, until all shall be usurped . . ."

The judicial supremacists have no regard for the processes of self-government. According to Robert Bork, the judges disdain the American people as "motivated by bigotry, racism, sexism, xenophobia, irrational sexual morality, and the like," and the judges see their mission as remaking our culture in their own liberal image.

The current situation is intolerable. We call on Congress to use its constitutional authority to restore the balance of power among the three branches. The accusation will be made that withdrawing jurisdiction from the federal courts is an attack on their power and indicates that we don't trust their decisions. That's exactly right; we don't, especially after *Roe, Casey, Romer, Lawrence, Kelo,* and *VanOrden,* the lower federal court decisions on the Pledge of Allegiance and pornography, and state court decisions on marriage and taxes. The judicial supremacists are out of control.

Despite public opinion polls showing overwhelming support for acknowledging God in the Pledge of Allegiance and other American traditions, supremacist doctrines continue to plague us without any relief in sight. The flawed *Lemon v. Kurtzman* test for the acknowledgment of God continues to encourage activist judges to hand down their own interpretations of what that test means. In 2004, the Supreme Court justices wrestled with the VMI grace-before-supper case (*Mellen v. Bunting*) during eight private weekly conferences before deciding *not* to decide the case, allowing the Fourth Circuit anti-God ruling to stand.

The ACLU is continuing its revenue-producing anti-God strategy in state after state. Many of the lawsuits are settled in the ACLU's favor and against the wishes of the people because the local units of government can't justify the costs of litigation and the risk of payment of the ACLU lawyers' fees. The settlements indicate tacit acquiescence in the false notion that the First Amendment prohibits the mention of God by any public official or in any public place.

Unless the American public makes its outrage about judicial supremacists loud and clear, the Supreme Court may believe it can continue to ignore the public. In the 1950s and 1960s, the American people and distinguished attorneys expressed public indignation about the Warren Court's anti-God, pro-criminal, pro-pornography, and pro-

Communist decisions. But Congress failed to take specific action, and later judges continued to expand on the powers grabbed by the Warren Court.

Congress has the duty to save us from judicial supremacists *and* from the harassment that is carried on by pressure groups litigating on the basis of supremacists' court rulings. Congress should act now.

The liberals who have lost their majority in Congress are using every procedural and rhetorical device to block reform of the runaway courts. They sanctimoniously assert that we must preserve an "independent" judiciary. What they really mean is a judiciary independent of the Constitution, and that's what we must not permit.

The histrionics of the liberals trying to retain their clutch on the courts reached a fever pitch when House Minority Leader Nancy Pelosi declaimed in the summer of 2005, "It is a decision of the Supreme Court. So this is almost as if God has spoken!" Her claim that the only way to counteract the Court's decisions is a constitutional amendment is just plain wrong. This book gives many constructive remedies to abolish the heresy that the Supreme Court has the rank of God.

On March 8, 2004, in Dallas, President Bush delivered the challenge: "We will not stand for judges who undermine democracy by legislating from the bench and try to remake the culture of America by court order."

The American people must demand that Congress use its full constitutional powers to protect America from judicial usurpation. This goal should take priority over everything else because the federal courts pose the number-one threat to our democratic process.

If we truly believe in self-government, ordinary Americans must take a major role in reforming the Imperial Judiciary. Private citizens must take an interest in court decisions, discuss them, comment on them, and ask television and radio talk shows to include them in their programming. Ordinary Americans must require every candidate for Congress to commit to restoring self-government by legislating historical limits to the federal judiciary's powers. Every candidate should commit to voting for legislation to remove the jurisdiction of the federal courts over those areas where we don't trust them, starting with the definition of marriage, the Pledge of Allegiance, the Ten Commandments, and the Boy Scouts.

Judicial supremacy is a heresy that has arisen and grown only during the last half century—it did not come to us from the Constitution or from America's rich heritage of respect for the rule of law. Judicial supremacy started with the Warren Supreme Court in the 1950s, and it has expanded to an intolerable level.

We must ask ourselves, what kind of a country do we want America to be? Do we want a country where "we the people" are sovereign, where we are governed by legislators we elect, where we can continue to raise our children in a land where the government respects our religious, cultural, and social traditions and heritage? Or will we be ruled by an unelected cadre of judges who are trampling on our most precious traditions and customs? The moral crisis of our nation is largely the result of court decisions that overturned longstanding laws and customs designed to protect morality, marriage, family integrity, and national security.

All those who love liberty must oppose judicial supremacy and its advocates. In the words of the Declaration of Independence, we must "disavow these Usurpations." The longer we delay in taking up the challenge, the harder it will be to achieve our goal. The truth of what has been done to us by judicial supremacists appears clearer every day. America faces a crisis of self-government.

Every session of the Supreme Court opens with the announcement: "God save the United States and this Honorable Court." The American people are crying out: "God save the United States *from* this Honorable Court."

Table of Cases

Excerpt from the Report of the American Bar Association Committee on Communist Tactics, Strategy, and Objectives, 1957

In the last 15 months the United States Supreme Court has decided 15 cases which directly affect the right of the United States of America to protect itself from Communist subversion:

1. *Communist Party v. Subversive Activities Control Board.* The Court refused to uphold or pass on the constitutionality of the Subversive Activities Control Act of 1950, and delayed the effectiveness of the Act.

2. *Pennsylvania v. Steve Nelson.* The Court held that it was unlawful for Pennsylvania to prosecute a Pennsylvania Communist Party leader under the Pennsylvania Sedition Act, and indicated that the anti sedition laws of 42 States and of Alaska and Hawaii cannot be enforced.

3. *Fourteen California Communists v. United States.* The Court reversed two federal courts and ruled that teaching and advocating forcible overthrow of our Government, even "with evil intent," was not punishable under the Smith Act as long as it was "divorced from any effort to instigate action to that

end," and ordered five Communist Party leaders freed and new trials for another nine.

4.   *Cole v. Young*. The Court reversed two federal courts and held that, although the Summary Suspension Act of 1950 gave the Federal Government the right to dismiss employees "in the interest of the national security of the United States," it was not in the interest of the national security to dismiss an employee who contributed funds and services to a not disputed subversive organization, unless that employee was in a "sensitive position."

5.   *Service v. Dulles*. The Court reversed two federal courts which had refused to set aside the discharge of John Stewart Service by the State Department. The FBI had a recording of a conversation between Service and an editor of the pro Communist magazine Amerasia, in the latter's hotel room in which Service spoke of military plans which were "very secret." Earlier the FBI had found large numbers of secret and confidential State Department documents in the Amerasia office. The lower courts had followed the McCarran amendment which gave the Secretary of State "absolute discretion" to discharge any employee "in the interests of the United States."

6.   *Slochower v. Board of Education of New York*. The Court reversed the decisions of three New York courts and held it was unconstitutional to automatically discharge a teacher, in accordance with New York law, because he took the Fifth Amendment when asked about Communist activities. On petition for rehearing, the Court admitted that its opinion was in error in stating that Slochower was not aware that his claim of the Fifth Amendment would ipso facto result in his discharge; however, the Court denied rehearing.

7. *Sweezy v. New Hampshire.* The Court reversed the New Hampshire Supreme Court and held that the Attorney General of New Hampshire was without authority to question Professor Sweezy, a lecturer at the State University, concerning a lecture and other suspected subversive activities. Questions which the Court said that Sweezy properly refused to answer included: "Did you advocate Marxism at that time?" and "Do you believe in Communism?"

8. *United States v. Witkovich.* The Court decided that, under the Immigration and Nationality Act of 1952, which provides that any alien against whom there is a final order of deportation shall "give information under oath as to his nationality, circumstances, habits, associations and activities and such other information, whether unrelated to the foregoing, as the Attorney General may deem fit and proper," the Attorney General did not have the right to ask Witkovich: "Since the order of deportation was entered in your case on June 25, 1953, have you attended any meetings of the Communist Party of the U.S.A.?"

9. *Schware v. Board of Bar Examiners of New Mexico.* The Court reversed the decisions of the New Mexico Board of Bar Examiners and of the New Mexico Supreme Court which had said: "We believe one who has knowingly given his loyalties to the Communist Party for six to seven years during a period of responsible adulthood is a person of questionable character." The Supreme Court substituted its judgment for that of New Mexico and ruled that "membership in the Communist Party during the 1930s cannot be said to raise substantial doubts about his present good moral character."

10. *Konigsberg v. State Bar of California.* The Court reversed the decisions of the California Committee of Bar Ex-

aminers and of the California Supreme Court and held that it was unconstitutional to deny a license to practice law to an applicant who refused to answer this question put by the Bar Committee: "Mr. Konigsberg, are you a Communist?" and a series of similar questions.

11. *Jencks v. United States.* The Court reversed two federal courts and held that Jencks, who was convicted of filing a false non Communist affidavit, must be given the contents of all confidential FBI reports which were made by any Government witness in the case even though Jencks "restricted his motions to a request for production of the reports to the trial judge for the judge's inspection and determination whether and to what extent the reports should be made available."

12. *Watkins v. United States.* The Court reversed the Federal District court and six judges of the Court of Appeals of the District of Columbia, and held that the House Un-American Activities Committee should not require a witness who admitted, "I freely cooperated with the Communist Party" to name his Communist associates, even though the witness did not invoke the Fifth Amendment. The Court said: "We remain unenlightened as to the subject to which the questions asked petitioner were pertinent."

13. *Raley, Stern and Brown v. Ohio.* The Court reversed the Ohio Supreme Court and lower courts and set aside the conviction of three men who had refused to answer questions about Communist activities put to them by the Ohio Un-American Activities Commission.

14. *Flaxner v. United States.* The Court reversed two federal courts and set aside the conviction of Flaxner of contempt for refusing to produce records of alleged Communist activities subpoenaed by the Senate Internal Security Subcommittee.

15.   *Sacher v. United States.* The Court reversed two federal courts and set aside the conviction of Sacher of contempt for refusing to tell the Senate Permanent Investigations Subcommittee whether he was or ever had been a Communist.

The *Communist Daily Worker* described the effect of these decisions as follows: "The Court delivered a triple barreled attack on (1) the Department of Justice and its Smith Act trials; (2) the free wheeling congressional inquisitions; and (3) the hateful loyalty security program of the Executive. Monday, June 17, is already a historic landmark . . . The curtain is closing on one of our worst periods."

Notes

1 *Judges Rewrite the Constitution*

- For an early use of the term "living Constitution," see "Mr. Justice Black and the Living Constitution," 76 *Harvard Law Review* 673 (1963).

- Justice William J. Brennan's November 21, 1982 speech was given at Park School, Baltimore, Maryland.

- Justice William O. Douglas's "wildcard" metaphor was quoted in "Are We Ready for Truth in Judging?" by W. Forrester, 63 *American Bar Association Journal* 1212 (1977).

- The legal doctrine of "substantive due process," and how it has been abused, is concisely explained in *The Tempting of America* by Robert H. Bork (Free Press, 1990), 31-32.

- The word "paradigm" was popularized by a 1962 philosophy book, *The Structure of Scientific Revolutions* by Thomas Kuhn. The book denied that scientific progress had a rational basis.

- The Jefferson quotation is from his Letter to William Johnson (June 12, 1823) in *Writings of Thomas Jefferson* 439, 449 (A. Lipscomb ed., 1904).

- Justice Scalia's "a country I do not recognize" is from his dissent in *Board of County Commissioners v. Umbehr* (1996).

- Robert H. Bork gives a useful definition of activist judges: "Activist judges are those who decide cases in ways that have no plausible connection to the law they purport to be applying, or who stretch or even contradict the meaning of that law. They arrive at results by announcing principles that were never contemplated by those who wrote and voted for the law. The law in question is usually a constitution, perhaps because the language of a constitution tends to be general and, in any event, judicial overreaching is then virtually immune to correction by the legislature or by the public." *Coercing Virtue: The Worldwide Rule of Judges* by Robert H. Bork (AEI Press, 2003), 8-9.

- Robert H. Bork wrote in a January 20, 2003, *Wall Street Journal* op-ed: "The Supreme Court has created a more permissive abortion regime than any state had enacted; prohibited any exercise or symbol of religion touching even remotely upon government; made the death penalty extremely difficult to impose and execute; disabled states from suppressing pornography; catered to the feminist agenda, including outlawing state all-male military schools; created a labyrinth of procedures making criminal prosecutions ever more difficult; used racial classifications to exclude children from their neighborhood public schools; perverted the political process by upholding campaign finance limits that shift political power to incumbents, journalists and labor unions; licensed the advocacy of violence and law violation; and protected as free speech computer-generated child pornography. These decisions are activist, i.e., not plausibly related to the actual Constitution."

2 *Judges Censor Acknowledgment of God*

- A list of the acknowledgments of God in all 50 state constitutions is in: *The Ten Commandments & Their Influence on American Law* by William J. Federer (Amerisearch, 2003), 52-55.

- No justice signed the Supreme Court's opinion expelling the Ten Commandments from schools in *Stone v. Graham*, which it issued in a per curiam decision. Nor did the Court allow oral argument or even full briefing in the case, as is customary. Instead, the Court simply banned the Ten Commandments outright based merely on a petition for certiorari, reversing the Kentucky judiciary. The Court decried that the posted Ten Commandments might "induce the schoolchildren to read, meditate upon, perhaps to venerate and obey, the Commandments." Many parents and teachers today wish that students would obey the Commandments and thereby restore order to our schools.

- Carter-appointed Judge Myron Thompson's judicial supremacy extends beyond the Ten Commandments case. For nineteen years, he has held control of a case alleging discrimination, inflicting enormous injury and costs on the State of Alabama (*Reynolds v. McInnes*, 2003). The Eleventh Circuit U.S. Court of Appeals reversed one of his decisions in that case and said this about his general handling of that case:

  "After 18 years of hearing following hearing, order after order, appeal and more appeals, it is fair to ask what has been accomplished and what remains to be done. The answer, it appears, is not enough has been accomplished and a lot remains to be done. This unwieldy litigation has been afflicting the judicial system and draining huge amounts of public funds from the State of Alabama for much too long. The amounts are staggering. Fifty million dollars in public funds has been spent on attorney's fees alone in the case. An additional $62.5 million has been paid out in consultant and expert costs, bringing the total litigation costs to the State of Alabama to more than $112 million, and that cost is growing at a rate of around $500,000.00 each and every month. The figure does not even include the close to $13 million in contempt fines that the State has paid and continues to pay at the rate of $250,000.00 per month. If the contempt fines are included in the total, the case has cost the taxpayers of the State of Alabama $125 million so far, and the tab is increasing at the rate of $750,000.00 per month."

Despite this rebuke, the case continues to run out of control and causes damages that are far in excess of what was alleged in the first place. By the end of 2004, Alabama had paid $174 million in expenses and fines on this case.

- Dean Griswold's speech was published in the *Washington Star*, March 3, 1963.

- The Court's hostility to religion started with nonbinding dicta in *Everson v. Board of Education* (1947). Justice Hugo Black wrote for the majority: "The 'establishment of religion' clause of the First Amendment means at least this: Neither a state nor the Federal Government can set up a church. Neither can pass laws which aid one religion, aid all religions, or prefer one religion over another."

  The decision itself permitted New Jersey to use tax money for school buses sending children to Catholic and other private schools, and was thus not particularly hostile to religion. But subsequent decisions have cited *Everson* dicta to argue that government cannot "aid all religions," and therefore must promote secularism. Justices Scalia and Thomas are the only ones on the current Supreme Court who acknowledge the errors in this reasoning. The Constitution was never intended to prohibit state policies that benefit all religions.

3 *Judges Redefine Marriage*

- The rejected federal Equal Rights Amendment (ERA) read: "Equality of rights under the law shall not be denied or abridged by the United States or by any State on account of sex." During the ten-year battle for ratification, 1972-1982, some ERA advocates denied that ERA would require the granting of marriage licenses to same-sex couples, but most legal scholars admitted this because the plain meaning of the amendment prohibits all discrimination "on account of sex." Senator Sam Ervin Jr., the leading constitutional lawyer in the U.S. Senate until his retirement, stated in Raleigh, NC (Feb. 22, 1977): "I don't know but one group of people in the United States the ERA would do any good for. That's homosexuals." Senator Ervin told the U.S. Senate that ERA's requirement to recognize same-sex marriages illustrates "the radical departures from our present system that the ERA will bring about in our society." He placed in the *Congressional Record* (Mar. 22, 1972) similar testimony by legal authorities Professor Paul Freund of the Harvard Law School and Professor James White of the Michigan Law School. This analysis was also supported in Perkins and Silverstein, "The Legality of Homosexual Marriage," 82 *Yale Law Journal* 573, 583-589 (Jan. 1973), and in the leading textbook on sex discrimination used in U.S. law schools, *Sex Discrimination and the Law* by Barbara A. Babcock, Ann Freedman, Eleanor Holmes Norton and Susan Ross (Little Brown, 1975).

• UCLA Professor Eugene Volokh's quote is at http://volokh.com/

• The text of Colorado's Amendment 2:

No Protected Status Based on Homosexual, Lesbian, or Bisexual Orientation.

Neither the State of Colorado, through any of its branches or departments, nor any of its agencies, political subdivisions, municipalities or school districts, shall enact, adopt or enforce any statute, regulation, ordinance or policy whereby homosexual, lesbian or bisexual orientation, conduct, practices or relationships shall constitute or otherwise be the basis of, or entitle any person or class of persons to have or claim any minority status, quota preferences, protected status or claim of discrimination. This Section of the Constitution shall be in all respects self-executing.

• The states where the voters passed state constitutional amendments to protect marriage as a relationship of a man and a woman are: Hawaii 1998, Alaska 1998, Nebraska 2000, Nevada 2002, Missouri 2004, Louisiana 2004, Arkansas 2004, Georgia 2004, Kentucky 2004, Michigan 2004, Mississippi 2004, Montana 2004, North Dakota 2004, Ohio 2004, Oklahoma 2004, Oregon 2004, Utah 2004, Kansas 2005, Texas 2005. These nineteen state constitutional amendments passed by an average of more than 70 percent, ranging from 57 percent in Oregon (where the same-sex marriage advocates carried on their most aggressive campaign) to 86 percent in Mississippi. The eleven amendments that were on the ballot in November 2004 all (except Utah) passed with a majority that was significantly larger than the vote for President Bush, which indicates that the power of this issue runs far deeper than party affiliation.

4 *Judges Undermine U.S. Sovereignty*

- Justice Breyer made his statement on ABC News on July 6, 2003.
- ABA president Alfred Carlton and Harvard Law School professor Laurence Tribe were quoted by CNSNews.com, July 11, 2003.

- Ginsburg is not known for her wit, but when she addressed the liberal lawyers of the American Constitution Society in August 2003, she managed to show her disdain for both President Bush and Chief Justice William Rehnquist with a triple entendre. Referring to Supreme Court decisions, she urged us to get rid of "the Lone Ranger mentality." First, this was a personal slap at Bush because he is closely associated with the word ranger: his baseball club was the Texas Rangers, and his top fundraisers are affectionately called Rangers. Second, Ginsburg's remark was a not-so-subtle sneer at Bush's foreign policy, which has been impudently criticized by snooty Europeans for its cowboy approach. Third, Ginsburg's comment sniped at Rehnquist, who had a small figurine of the Lone Ranger in his office, reminding him of the years when he was the lone conservative on the Supreme Court. Ginsburg's Lone Ranger metaphor was characteristically feminist, as the feminists despise everything masculine, and Rangers are very masculine. Ginsburg's speech to the American Constitution Society was reported by the Associated Press, Aug. 3, 2003, and by MSNBC on Aug. 4, 2003.

- The comment about Margaret Marshall is from "A Bold Stroke" by Emily Bazelton, *Legal Affairs*, May-June 2004.

- The European Court of Human Rights decision granting voting rights to prisoners was *Hirst v. The United Kingdom* (No. 2) issued on March 30, 2004.

- For news of the NAFTA Chapter 11 decisions, see the *New York Times*, April 19, 2004.

- Robert H. Bork's book, *Coercing Virtue: The Worldwide Rule of Judges* (AEI Press, 2003), is an excellent account of how judges worldwide are setting themselves up as the ruling class.

5 *Judges Threaten Property Rights*

- John Adams' quotation is from *The Works of John Adams, Second President of the United States*, Charles Francis Adams, editor (Boston: Charles C. Little and James Brown, 1851), vol. VI, 9.

- Michigan finally repudiated its own decision in the *Poletown* case. The Michigan supreme court held in *County of Wayne v. Hathcock* (2004) that the U.S. Supreme Court's *Berman* decision had no bearing on Michigan's interpretation of its state constitution to protect private property owners.

6 *Judges Promote Pornography*

- Judge Bork's statement about the "vulgarity of popular culture" is from his book *Coercing Virtue: The Worldwide Rule of Judges* (AEI Press, 2003), 64.

- The decision by Justice Brennan that opened the floodgates to pornography in 1966 was *A Book Named "John Cleland's Memoirs of a Woman of Pleasure" v. Massachusetts*. That was followed by thirty-four per curiam (anonymous) decisions overturning

lower court decisions, and another signed decision covering
two additional cases. These decisions, all issued between 1966
and 1970, awarded victories to the pornographers.

Per curiam decisions:

1. *Redmond v. United States*, 384 U.S. 264 (1966)
2. *Potomac News Co. v. United States*, 389 U.S. 47 (1967)
3. *Conner v. Hammond*, 389 U.S. 48 (1967)
4. *Central Magazine Sales, Ltd. v. United States*, 389 U.S. 50 (1967)
5. *Chance v. California*, 389 U.S. 89 (1967)
6. *Keney v. New York*, 388 U.S. 440 (1967)
7. *Friedman v. New York*, 388 U.S. 441 (1967)
8. *Ratner v. California*, 388 U.S. 442 (1967)
9. *Cobert v. New York*, 388 U.S. 443 (1967)
10. *Sheperd v. New York*, 388 U.S. 444 (1967)
11. *Avansino v. New York*, 388 U.S. 446 (1967)
12. *Aday v. United States*, 388 U.S. 447 (1967)
13. *Corinth Publications, Inc. v. Wesberry*, 388 U.S. 448 (1967)
14. *Rosenbloom v. Virginia*, 388 U.S. 450 (1967)
15. *A Quantity of Copies of Books v. Kansas*, 388 U.S. 452 (1967)
16. *Schackman v. California*, 388 U.S. 454 (1967)
17. *Books, Inc. v. United States*, 388 U.S. 449 (1967)
18. *Mazes v. Ohio*, 388 U.S. 453 (1967)
19-21. *Redrup v. New York*, 386 U.S. 767 (1967) (three cases)
22. *Felton v. Pensacola*, 390 U.S. 340 (1968)
23. *Rabeck v. New York*, 391 U.S. 462 (1968)
24. *I. M. Amusement Corp. v. Ohio*, 389 U.S. 573 (1968)
25. *Robert Arthur Management Corp. v. Tennessee*, 389 U.S. 578 (1968)
26. *Lee Art Theatre, Inc. v. Virginia*, 392 U.S. 636 (1968)
27. *Henry v. Louisiana*, 392 U.S. 655 (1968)
28. *Teitel Film Corp. v. Cusack*, 390 U.S. 139 (1968)
29. *Carlos v. New York*, 396 U.S. 119 (1969)
30. *Von Cleef v. New Jersey*, 395 U.S. 814 (1969)
31. *Bloss v. Dykema*, 398 U.S. 278 (1970)
32. *Cain v. Kentucky*, 397 U.S. 319 (1970)

33. *Walker v. Ohio*, 398 U.S. 434 (1970)

34. *Hoyt v. Minnesota*, 399 U.S. 524 (1970)

Signed decision:

Interstate Circuit, Inc. v. Dallas, 390 U.S. 676 (1968) (two cases)

- The Supreme Court had long upheld laws against obscenity until President Lyndon B. Johnson appointed his personal lawyer Abe Fortas to the Court as an associate justice in 1965. Fortas then voted for pornographers in the series of Court decisions in 1966 and 1967 that changed U.S. law on pornography and flooded the country with lewd materials that previously had been available only on the black market. In one of his decisions in favor of pornographers, Fortas voted to reverse the conviction of a corporate publisher of pornography, William Hamling, who had been a Fortas client. Hamling had paid Fortas a fee to get a valuable second-class mailing permit for his lewd magazine. Hamling once bragged that he had hired Abe Fortas as his attorney because Fortas "could fix anything no matter who was in power." When Chief Justice Earl Warren announced his resignation on June 26, 1968, LBJ nominated Fortas to be Chief Justice. In a dramatic confirmation battle that fall, the Senate rejected Fortas's promotion to Chief Justice primarily because of his conflicts of interest involving pornographers. The revelations during the confirmation process resulted in Fortas's resignation as Associate Justice of the Supreme Court on May 14, 1969.

  Warren's announcement of his resignation (which was to become effective only on confirmation of his successor) was planned so that President Johnson could appoint the new chief justice, rather than Richard Nixon who was expected to be elected in November 1968 (and whom Warren hated). After the Senate refused to confirm LBJ's choice of Fortas, Warren served another term, and Nixon appointed Warren Burger in 1969.

- The Supreme Court entertained so many obscenity cases that Bob Woodward's 1979 book, *The Brethren*, described a regular

"movie day," when the justices and clerks would watch pornographic movies related to cases under consideration.

7 Judges Foster Feminism

• Ruth Bader Ginsburg co-authored the book called *Sex Bias in
the U.S. Code* in 1977 with another feminist, Brenda Feigen-
Fasteau, for which they were paid with federal funds under
Contract No. CR3AKO10. The 230-page book was published by
the U.S. Commission on Civil Rights. It was written to identify
the federal laws that allegedly discriminate on account of sex
and to promote ratification of the then-pending federal Equal
Rights Amendment (ERA), for which Ginsburg was a fervent
advocate. Here are some of Ginsburg's radical feminist recommendations set forth in her book *Sex Bias in the U.S. Code.*

Ginsburg called for the sex-integration of prisons and re-
formatories so that conditions of imprisonment, security and
housing could be equal. She explained, "If the grand design of
such institutions is to prepare inmates for return to the community as persons equipped to benefit from and contribute to
civil society, then perpetuation of single-sex institutions should
be rejected." (101) She called for the sex-integration of Boy
Scouts and Girl Scouts because they "perpetuate stereotyped
sex roles." (145) She insisted on sex-integrating "college frater-
nity and sorority chapters" and replacing them with "college
social societies." (169) She even cast constitutional doubt on
the legality of "Mother's Day and Father's Day as separate
holidays." (146)

Ginsburg called for reducing the age of consent for sexual
acts to persons who are "less than 12 years old." (102) She asserted that laws against "bigamists, persons cohabiting with
more than one woman, and women cohabiting with a biga-
mist" are unconstitutional. (195) She objected to laws against
prostitution because "prostitution, as a consensual act between
adults, is arguably within the zone of privacy protected by
recent constitutional decisions." (97) Ginsburg wrote that the
Mann Act (which punishes those who engage in interstate sex

traffic of women and girls) is "offensive." Such acts should be considered "within the zone of privacy." (98)

Ginsburg's view of the traditional family was radical feminist. She said that the concept of husband-breadwinner and wife-homemaker "must be eliminated from the code if it is to reflect the equality principle," (206) and she called for "a comprehensive program of government supported child care." (214)

She demanded that we "firmly reject draft or combat exemption for women," stating that "women must be subject to the draft if men are." But, she added, "the need for affirmative action and for transition measures is particularly strong in the uniformed services." (218)

An indefatigable censor, Ginsburg listed hundreds of "sexist" words that must be eliminated from all statutes. Among words she found offensive were: man, woman, manmade, mankind, husband, wife, mother, father, sister, brother, son, daughter, serviceman, longshoreman, postmaster, watchman, seamanship, and "to man" (a vessel). (15-16) She even wanted he, she, him, her, his, and hers to be dropped down the Memory Hole. They must be replaced by he/she, her/him, and hers/his, and federal statutes must use the bad grammar of "plural constructions to avoid third person singular pronouns." (52-53)

It's too bad that Americans were denied the entertainment of a c-span broadcast of a Senate Judiciary Committee interrogation of Ginsburg about her out-of-the-mainstream views. But the Republicans rolled over and Ginsburg was confirmed as a Supreme Court justice 96 to 3.

• Sandra Day O'Connor's voting record in the Arizona State Senate includes the following: On April 29, 1970, she voted Yes on h.b. 20, an abortion-on-demand bill, in the Senate Judiciary Committee. On April 30, 1970, she voted Yes on the same bill in the Republican Majority Caucus (where the bill was defeated). On April 23, 1974, she voted No in the Senate Judiciary Committee on a Right to Life Memorial asking Congress to extend constitutional protections to the unborn. On Feb. 8, 1973, she co-sponsored the Family Planning Act (s.b. 1190) to provide "family planning," including abortions, to minors without parental consent. In May 1974, she voted No on an amendment to prohibit abortions at the taxpayer-supported University of Arizona Hospital. On March 23, 1972, she co-sponsored the Equal Rights Amendment (which Arizona consistently rejected). On April 15, 1971, she succeeded in amending anti-pornography bills (h.b. 301 & 302) so that porn shops ("adult bookstores") could be 4,000 feet from schools and parks instead of at least a mile away. In 1973, she sponsored Arizona's no-fault divorce bill (h.b. 1007).

8 *Judges Handicap Law Enforcement*

• In *Furman v. Georgia*, the Supreme Court invalidated capital punishment in Georgia and Texas and effectively overturned death penalty statutes everywhere else in the country. At least 41 jurisdictions were directly affected. The impact of this unprecedented decision was staggering. In Florida alone, the *Furman* decision had the effect of voiding 102 executions of criminals convicted of heinous crimes.

Despite overwhelming public support for the death penalty, California was unable to execute a single convicted murderer between 1967 and 1992, when Robert Alton Harris was finally sent to the gas chamber. He had killed two teenagers and finished off their half-eaten hamburgers afterwards. On parole for voluntary manslaughter when he murdered them, he reportedly laughed about his killing spree and did not dispute his guilt. Yet attorneys and courts delayed his original execution date in 1981 for over ten years, until finally the U.S. Supreme Court itself felt compelled to withdraw jurisdiction over the case from all lower federal courts in *Vasquez v. Harris* (1992).

9 *Judges Invite Illegal Immigration*

• The Citizenship Clause in federal law is Section 1401(a) of Title 8 of the United States Code.

- Mexico is just one of many countries from which visitors now come to the United States and claim birthright citizenship. "An entire cottage industry now caters to people from South Korea, China, the Middle East and elsewhere who visit the United States just to give birth and then go back home. Once the child reaches 21, he can petition to have his families outside the country join him legally in the United States. These children are called 'anchor babies.'" "Immigration: Stop the Abuse," *Florida Times-Union* (Jacksonville), April 4, 2003, B-4. Some estimates are that anchor babies exceed 200,000 each year. Websites even promote travel to the United States to give birth, setting up a claim to American citizenship.

- By the government's own estimates, in January 2000 there were seven million illegal aliens living in the United States. "Estimates of the Unauthorized Immigrant Population Residing in the United States: 1990 to 2000," Office of Policy and Planning, U.S. Immigration and Naturalization Service 1 (2003). A Bear Stearns report dated January 3, 2005, stated: "The number of illegal immigrants in the United States may be as high as 20 million people." Tens of thousands pour over our border on a daily basis.

- Rice University economist Dr. Donald Huddle estimated that illegal aliens cost $5.4 billion in public assistance as long ago as 1990. Shari B. Fallek, "Comment: Health Care for Illegal Aliens: Why It Is a Necessity," 19 *Houston Journal of International Law*, 951, 957 (Spring 1997). "For the decade from 1993 to 2002, he estimated that the net cost for illegal immigrants would be $186.4 billion. Between 1993 and 2002, illegal immigrants will cost $221.5 billion in public assistance and displacement costs. Regarding jobs, Dr. Huddle suggested that in 1992, 2.07 million U.S. workers were displaced from jobs by immigrants, which cost $11.9 billion. He estimated the cost of job displacement for the 1993-2002 decade to be $171.5 billion." Id. at 957-58.

- *Clayworth v. Bonta* noted that California medical programs pay an estimated $852 million annually to cover the costs of illegal aliens. For diseases brought in by aliens, see Dr. Madeleine Pelner Cosman, "Illegal Aliens and American Medicine," 10 *Journal of American Physicians and Surgeons*, No. 1, 6 (Spring 2005).

10 *Judges Interfere with Elections*

• The Supreme Court is on the verge of reentering the political thicket of reapportionment in a major way. In *Vieth v. Jubelirer* (2004), the Supreme Court reviewed reapportionment in Pennsylvania, where it had been alleged that the majority party redrew the district boundaries in order to favor themselves. Four justices agreed that political gerrymandering claims are nonjusticiable because no judicially discernible and manageable standards for adjudicating such claims exist. Justice Kennedy seemed to agree, as he said: "Because there are yet no agreed upon substantive principles of fairness in districting, we have no basis on which to define clear, manageable, and politically neutral standards for measuring the particular burden a given partisan classification imposes on representational rights."

But that doesn't make it hopeless for a supremacist such as Kennedy, as he went on to say: "It is not in our tradition to foreclose the judicial process from the attempt to define standards and remedies where it is alleged that a constitutional right is burdened or denied. Nor is it alien to the Judiciary to draw or approve election district lines. . . . Our willingness to enter the political thicket of the apportionment process with respect to one-person, one-vote claims makes it particularly difficult to justify a categorical refusal to entertain claims against this other type of gerrymandering."

Kennedy and the other supremacist justices seem to invite future cases that would give the Court the opportunity to invent new standards for reviewing and redoing apportionment decisions. Justices Stevens, Souter, and Breyer each have their own ideas for what those standards might be. For example, Breyer wants to review and reverse "the unjustified use of political factors to entrench a minority in power."

Political reapportionment is often hotly contentious and subject to political deal-making, but it won't be improved by turning it over to judges who cannot even identify the criteria that they would use for drawing district lines.

- How a court-ordered recount of the Florida ballots in 2000 might have turned out has been a matter of some speculation, as it is difficult to predict what standards the courts would have used once they abandoned the pre-election standards. One group of newspaper reporters led by *USA Today* concluded (May 11, 2001): "Who would have won if Al Gore had gotten the manual counts he requested in four counties? Answer: George W. Bush. Who would have won if the U.S. Supreme Court had not stopped the hand recount of undervotes, which are ballots that registered no machine-readable vote for president? Answer: Bush, under three of four standards. Who would have won if all disputed ballots—including those rejected by machines because they had more than one vote for president—had been recounted by hand? Answer: Bush, under the two most widely used standards; Gore, under the two least used." Thus, Bush probably would have won a court-ordered recount, but Florida judges could have manipulated the outcome to make it appear that Gore won.

- Regarding the sales pitch for touch-screen voting machines: The core logic behind the Ninth Circuit ruling was based on the Berkeley study. The study was funded by Sequoia Voting Systems, a major provider of touch-screen voting machines, which is actively seeking additional contracts to install its equipment in California counties.

- As the ballots were being counted after a statewide election in Alabama in 1994, it appeared that the first Republican would be elected to the state supreme court since Reconstruction days. With a few thousand absentee ballots still uncounted and Republican Perry Hooper appearing to be ahead, the Democrats rushed into court to ask a judge to change the rules. The Alabama statute was very clear that the absentee ballots had to be notarized by the voter in order to be counted, and that procedure had been followed for years. The Democrats demanded that the court rewrite the law and eliminate that requirement. The Democrats kept the case in court for a year, trying to get judicial supremacists to order the counting of illegal ballots. Finally, the Eleventh Circuit U.S. Court of Appeals upheld the law in *Roe v. State of Alabama* and allowed Perry Hooper to take his seat as chief justice of the state supreme court.

11 *Judges Take Over Parents' Rights*

- The figures on custodial parents and children, and on 85 percent of custodial parents being women, are from U.S. Census Bureau, Current Population Reports, Oct. 2003.

- The $40 billion figure for support payments in 2002 is from U.S. Census Bureau News, Feb. 25, 2005.

- The right of parents to authority and autonomy in the rearing of their children traditionally enjoyed consensus in the United States. This principle—that "parents have a fundamental constitutional right to rear their children, including the right to determine who shall educate and socialize them"—was unanimously reaffirmed by the U.S. Supreme Court in 2000 in *Troxel v. Granville*. This was a case of grandparents who sought visitation with their grandchildren over the opposition of the surviving parent. The Supreme Court invalidated a Washington State statute that gave judges the power to order visitation of children on "a best-interests-of-the-child standard." The statute placed hardly any limit on a judge's discretion to award visitation whenever he thought he could make a better decision than a child's parent. The justices split on that issue, but both majority and dissenting justices unanimously upheld the principle that "parents have a fundamental constitutional right to rear their children, including the right to determine who shall educate and socialize them," citing the famous cases of *Pierce v. Society of Sisters* (1925) and *Meyer v. Nebraska* (1923). Justice O'Connor's plurality opinion (joined by Rehnquist, Ginsburg and Breyer) explained: ". . . the Washington statute places the best-interest determination solely in the hands of the judge. Should the judge disagree with the parent's estimation of the child's best interests, the judge's view necessarily prevails." Rebutting this error and the lower court judge's argument that "I think [visitation with grandparents Troxel] would be in the best interest of the children," O'Connor wrote: "The decisional framework employed by the Superior Court directly contravened the traditional presumption that a fit parent will act in the best interest of his or her child. . . . The court's presumption failed to provide any protection for [parent] Granville's fundamental constitutional right to make decisions concerning the rearing of her own daughters."

• Parents' rights are not only protected by the U.S. Constitution, but are also recognized as a fundamental principle of state law. Citing both federal and state constitutions, a New York appellate court ruled in *Alfonso v. Fernandez* (1993) that parents' fundamental rights are violated when public schools distribute condoms to high school students without their parents' consent. The court's opinion said that parents "enjoy a well-recognized liberty interest in rearing and educating their children in accord with their own views. Intrusion into the relationship between parent and child requires a showing of an overriding necessity." The court noted that "At common law it was for parents to consent or withhold their consent to the rendition of health services to their children." When public schools with compulsory attendance dispensed condoms to children without their parents' consent, the court found that parents were "being forced to surrender a parenting right—specifically, to influence and guide the sexual activity of their children without State interference."

• In *Parham v. J.R.* (1979), Justice Potter Stewart wrote: "For centuries it has been a canon of the common law that parents speak for their minor children. So deeply imbedded in our traditions is this principle of law that the Constitution itself may compel a State to respect it."

• Public schools began to take over parenting authority and duties in the 1970s. This change was best capsuled by the Honorable Samuel I. Hayakawa, former president of San Francisco State College, when he was a U.S. Senator from California: "An educational heresy has flourished, a heresy that rejects the idea of education as the acquisition of knowledge and skills . . . the heresy of which I speak regards the fundamental task in education as therapy."

• Resolutions passed by the National Education Association at its 2005 national convention assert the power of public school personnel over parents in numerous areas of curriculum. For example, Resolution B-42 states: "Sex Education. The Association recognizes that the public school must assume an increasingly important role in providing the instruction. Teachers and health professionals must be qualified to teach in this area and must be legally protected from censorship and lawsuits. The Association also believes that to facilitate the realization of human potential, it is the right of every individual to live in an environment of freely available information and knowledge about sexuality and encourages affiliates and members to support appropriately established sex education programs. Such programs should include information on sexual abstinence, birth control and family planning, diversity of culture, diversity of sexual orientation and gender identification, parenting skills, prenatal care, sexually transmitted diseases, incest, sexual abuse, sexual harassment, homophobia." [In this resolution, "every individual" includes children of every age starting with pre-kindergarten, and "censorship" is the word the NEA commonly uses to describe parents' efforts to protect the morals and values of their own children.] Resolution B-1 states: "Early Childhood Education. The National Education Association supports early child education programs in the public schools for children from birth through age eight."

- *Scientific American Mind* (October 2005, 65-67) published a paper by psychologists Robert E. Emery, Randy K. Otto and William O'Donohue, entitled "Custody Disputed," which states: "Our own thorough evaluation of tests that purport to pick the 'best parent,' the 'best interests of the child' or the 'best custody arrangement' reveals that they are wholly inadequate. No studies examining their effectiveness have ever been published in a peer-reviewed journal. Because there is simply no psychological science to support them, the tests should not be used. . . . Court tests that expert evaluators use to gauge the supposed best interests of a child should be abandoned. . . . The coupling of the vague 'best interest of the child' standards with the American adversarial justice system puts judges in the position of trying to perform an impossible task: making decisions that are best for children using a procedure that is not. . . . We believe it is legally, morally and scientifically wrong to make custody evaluators de facto decision makers, which they often are because judges typically accept an evaluator's recommendation. Parents should determine their children's lives after separation, just as when they are married. . . . Parents—not judges or mental health professionals—are the best experts on their own children. We are simply urging the same rigor that is applied to expert testimony in all other legal proceedings." *See also*, "For Arbiters in Custody Battles, Wide Power and Little Scrutiny" by Leslie Eaton, *New York Times*, May 23, 2004.

- The California statute states: "The mother of an unemancipated minor child and the father, if presumed to be the father under Section 7611, are equally entitled to the custody of the child." California Family Code, sect. 3010(a). Such provisions are generally ignored by family courts, which order custody based on the judge's opinion of the best interest of the child.

- California's attempt to define "best interest" says that the court should consider whatever factors it finds relevant, including "the health, safety, and welfare of the child" and a few other factors. Michigan lists twelve factors, starting with "the love, affection, and other emotional ties existing between the parties involved and the child." The statutes offer no clue as to how these factors should be measured or weighted.

- The famous 1965 Daniel Patrick Moynihan report, "The Negro Family: The Case for National Action," warned that the rise in single-mother families was no harmless lifestyle choice, but was unraveling "the basic socializing unit" and causing high rates of delinquency, joblessness, school failure and male alienation. Moynihan was bitterly attacked for speaking what is now universally recognized as the awful truth. Kay S. Hymowitz, in the Manhattan Institute's *City Journal* (August 2005, 12-23) wrote that Moynihan's critics romanticized female-headed families as a good thing. She described how the feminists, who were fixated on notions of patriarchal oppression, claimed that criticism of mother-headed households was really an effort to deny women their independence, their sexuality, or both.

- The Census Bureau reports that 31 percent of children do not live in a home with two parents, based on a non-legal definition that includes stepparents. The more accurate and widely used statistic is that 40 percent of children live in homes without their own two parents.

- The *Illinois Bar Journal*, June 2005, 290ff., explained how women use court-issued restraining orders as a tool for the mother to get sole child custody and to bar the father from visitation. In big type, the magazine proclaimed: "Orders of protection are designed to prevent domestic violence, but they can also become part of the gamesmanship of divorce." The "game" is that mothers can assert falsehoods or trivial marital complaints and thereby get sole-custody orders which deprive children of their fathers based on the presumption (popularized by the radical feminists) that men are abusers of women. The article states that restraining orders, which courts "customarily" issue at an "ex parte hearing without testimony," actually "make the case ineligible for mediation," "limit settlement options," and mean that "joint parenting is not an option."

- Researchers Margaret F. Brinig and Douglas W. Allen explain how the typical pattern of giving primary custody to the mother deprives the father not only of his time with his children but also all of his authority and decision-making in the rearing of his children: "If the court names her primary custodian, she makes most, if not all, of the major decisions regarding the child. As custodial parent, she will be able to spend the money the husband pays in child support exactly as she pleases—something she may not do during marriage. Finally, although the court will usually have ordered visitation she can exert some control over her former husband by regulating many, although not all, aspects of the time he spends with the child. In the extreme, she can even 'poison' the child against the father." "These Boots Are Made for Walking: Why Most Divorce Filers Are Women," 2 *American Law and Economics Review* 126 (Spring 2000).

- The preponderance of academic research shows that shared parenting is superior to single-parent custody by all available measures. Meta-analyses of the research can be found in *Father and Child Reunion* by Warren Farrell (Penguin, 2001) and in "Child Adjustment in Joint-Custody Versus Sole-Custody Arrangements: A Meta-Analytic Review" by Robert Bauserman, *Journal of Family Psychology*, 2002, Vol. 16, No. 1, 91102. One of the benefits of shared parenting is that it reduces court involvement and litigation. Nevertheless, unscientific ideology-driven arguments that are lacking in common sense continue to be highly publicized. For example, see Peggy Drexler, *Raising Boys Without Men: How Maverick Moms Are Creating the Next Generation of Exceptional Men* (Rodale, 2005), which makes the argument that single mother and lesbian homes are the best environments for boys.

- Divorce law is now commonly called no-fault. This radical change in divorce law, which took place in the 1970s, made it possible for either party to unilaterally walk out of the marriage contract without asserting fault by the other spouse, but courts definitely consider fault in determining child custody.

The domestic-violence lobby has implemented the use of a long litany of new and ill-defined (including non-physical) faults against spouses that can be invoked by the courts in deciding the terms of child custody. As a result, divorce proceedings are often much more bitter and contentious than ever before.

12 *Judges Impose Taxes*

- The Nevada supreme court decision was severely criticized in "Recent Cases," 117 *Harvard Law Review* 972 (Jan. 2004), which concluded that the decision "poses a serious threat to the separation of powers."

- *Las Vegas Review* columnist Vin Suprynowicz (July 20, 2003) wrote that the crucial Nevada supreme court decision was decided long before the lawsuit was actually filed. Citing a retired Nevada judge, Suprynowicz wrote that Governor Guinn spoke with Justices Bob Rose and Miriam Shearing at the beginning of the budget battle and received assurances from them that the Nevada supreme court would impose his proposed tax hikes. They even predicted that it would be a 6 to 1 vote, which turned out to be the exact outcome of the Nevada supreme court decision. The U.S. Supreme Court declined to hear an appeal of the case.

- An especially egregious example of judicial usurpation of legislative power occurred in Yonkers, New York, in 1988. When the Yonkers city council voted 4 to 3 not to ratify a court ordered plan to build rent-subsidized multi-family housing in a predominately white neighborhood, federal district judge Leonard Sand slapped huge fines on the individual members of the city council who had voted against the judge's plan. After the individual fines had been upheld by the Second Circuit U.S. Court of Appeals, the city adopted the judge's plan in the face of daily fines of $1 million. The Supreme Court rejected the personal fines on narrow technical grounds in a 5 to 4 decision. *Spallone v. United States* (1990).

- James E. Ryan's comment: University of Virginia Legal Working Paper Series, June 22, 2005.

13 How Judicial Supremacy Began

- This law review article gives some of the history of *Marbury v. Madison*: "There is, then, no doctrine of national, substantive judicial supremacy which inexorably flows from *Marbury v. Madison* itself, i.e., no doctrine that the only interpretation of the Constitution which all branches of the national government must employ is the interpretation which the Court may provide in the course of litigation." "A Critical Guide to *Marbury v. Madison*" by William W. Van Alstyne, 18 *Duke Law Journal* 1-47 (1969).

- Jefferson's "obiter dissertation" comment is from his letter to Justice William Johnson, Monticello, June 12, 1823.

- The concept of judicial review has a strong form and a weak form. The weak form of judicial review occurs when, in the course of deciding a specific case, a court construes a statute in the light of a superior interpretation of the Constitution. The strong form of judicial review consists of using the Constitution (or previous judicial interpretations of it) to override the plain text meaning of a statute, and construing the statute as it might apply hypothetically to entities that are not parties to the case before the court. Chief Justice John Marshall only gave us the weak form of judicial review. He had nothing to do with the strong form of judicial review so prevalent today. This book is concerned with the strong form of judicial supremacy and concludes that it has become entrenched in American government only recently. See the law review article by Brian M. Feldman, "Evaluating Public Endorsement of the Weak and Strong Forms of Judicial Supremacy," 89 *Virginia Law Review* 979 (2003), which argues that the American public has never endorsed the strong form of judicial supremacy, and that such an endorsement would be essential to its legitimacy.

- The notion of judicial supremacy should not be confused with federal supremacy. Federal supremacy is the principle that federal laws override or preempt state and local laws, but only in the use of the federal government's delegated powers as defined by the Constitution.

- The opposition to judicial supremacy by Jefferson and Lincoln is explained in "Lincoln on Judicial Despotism" by Robert P. George, *First Things*, Feb. 2003, 130: 36-40.

14 *How Judicial Supremacy Grew*

- *U.S. News & World Report* published the text of the ABA *Report on Communist Tactics, Strategy and Objectives*, Aug. 16, 1957, p. 135. The 1958 report of the same ABA committee, which was very similar, was placed in the *Congressional Record* by Senator Styles Bridges on Aug. 22, 1958, and again by Senator Everett Dirksen on March 1, 1962.

- Senator James O. Eastland's analysis of the Warren Court was published in *U.S. News & World Report*, July 18, 1958, 81.

- Justice Brennan took the judicial supremacy of *Cooper v. Aaron* to new extremes when he invoked the "spirit" of a statute in order to violate its express language and thereby embrace the use of quotas in a hiring agreement (*United Steelworkers v. Weber*, 1979). That led Rehnquist in dissent to mock Justice Brennan's decision as "a tour de force reminiscent not of jurists such as Hale, Holmes, and Hughes, but of escape artists such as Houdini." Since then, thirty court opinions have questioned, criticized or distinguished the supremacist ruling in *Steelworkers*.

- The Latin phrase obiter dicta (meaning words said in passing, or by the way) is used to describe extraneous parts of a court opinion. This is often abbreviated as dicta (meaning words). Sometimes the words help explain the decision or are otherwise informative, but they aren't necessary to reach the conclusion. Law schools used to teach courses in "Legal Method" or "Elements of the Law" in which students were taught to distinguish and disregard dicta as nonbinding and non-precedential. However, the Warren Court popularized reliance on dicta so much that those courses aren't even taught any more. Thomas Jefferson used a variation of the phrase obiter dicta when he called *Marbury v. Madison* an "obiter dissertation."

• Judicial supremacy is promoted with various myths and misconceptions about the history of the Court. For example, Justice Stephen Breyer gave a speech to a 2001 American Bar Association meeting, citing two cases he thought were particularly instructive. He was trying to teach the lesson that poor defenseless people need judicial supremacy, and that America would be a better place if the other branches of government took their policy orders from the Supreme Court.

Referring to the 1832 Cherokee Indian case (*Worcester v. Georgia*), Breyer said that thousands of Indians died because Andrew Jackson refused to enforce a Supreme Court order. Referring to *Cooper v. Aaron*, Breyer said that Eisenhower enforced the court order by sending federal troops so that black children could attend good schools.

But Justice Breyer's facts are completely wrong. The Supreme Court in 1832 ruled only in favor of a couple of white missionaries, not the Cherokees. Jackson did not defy a Supreme Court decision. Several thousand Cherokees did die, but that had nothing to do with any Supreme Court decision and it happened six or seven years later after Jackson left office.

Breyer said that Eisenhower sent troops to enforce *Cooper v. Aaron*. In reality, Eisenhower sent the troops in 1957 and withdrew the troops at the end of the school year in 1958, before *Cooper v. Aaron* was decided. The Arkansas schools were being desegregated. Then, *Cooper v. Aaron* threw the Little Rock schools into such chaos that the high schools were closed for the entire 1958-59 academic year.

Of course, Breyer likes *Cooper v. Aaron* because it was the first statement of judicial supremacy since *Dred Scott* in 1857, but that is no excuse for getting the facts wrong. It appears that the whole basis for his belief in judicial supremacy is in these myths.

15 *How To Stop Judicial Supremacy*

- For a history of the filibuster and a road map for how the Senate can adopt new rules by a simple majority vote, see "The Constitutional Option to Change Senate Rules and Procedures: A Majoritarian Means to Overcome the Filibuster" by Martin B. Gold & Dimple Gupta, *Harvard Journal of Law & Public Policy*, vol. 28, pp. 205-272 (Winter 2005).

- The Daschle law about brush clearing is Public Law 107-206, Sec. 706(j), which states: "Any action authorized by this section shall not be subject to judicial review by any court of the United States." The law authorized the Interior Department to clear timber in the Black Hills of South Dakota in order to fight and prevent forest fires. Environmental groups had filed several lawsuits to stop timber clearing. At least one court had issued an order and other suits were pending. The Daschle law terminated all these suits so that timber clearing could continue without judicial interference. The constitutionality of Congress terminating those lawsuits has not been questioned.

- Chief Justice Oliver Ellsworth had served as a member of the Committee of Detail at the Constitutional Convention, which drafted the provision in Article III authorizing Congress to limit the jurisdiction of the Supreme Court. Chief Justice Ellsworth wrote in *Wiscart v. Dauchy* (1796): "The Constitution, distributing the judicial power of the United States, vests in the Supreme Court, an original as well as an appellate jurisdiction. The original jurisdiction, however, is confined to cases affecting ambassadors, other public ministers and consuls, and those in which a State shall be a party. In all other cases, only an appellate jurisdiction is given to the court; and even the appellate jurisdiction is, likewise, qualified; inasmuch as it is given 'with such exceptions, and under such regulations, as the Congress shall make.' Here then, is the ground, and the only ground, on which we can sustain an appeal. If Congress has provided no rule to regulate our proceedings, we cannot exercise an appellate jurisdiction; and if the rule is provided, we cannot depart from it. The question, therefore, on the constitutional point of an appellate jurisdiction, is simply, whether Congress has established any rule for regulating its exercise?"

• Many of the Supreme Court's decisions that are deplorable—because they are legislating from the bench and remaking our culture by court order—are based on the Fourteenth Amendment. The U.S. Constitution gives Congress, not the Court, the power to enforce the Fourteenth Amendment. Section 5 states: "The Congress shall have power to enforce, by appropriate legislation, the provisions of this article."

John G. Roberts' 27-page document, written when he was Special Assistant to the Attorney General during the Reagan Administration, makes this additional argument in support of Congress's constitutional power: "Congress may derive additional authority in regulating Supreme Court appellate jurisdiction over Fourteenth Amendment cases by virtue of section 5 of that Amendment . . . Congress could invoke the authority of this section in divesting the Supreme Court of appellate jurisdiction over specified Fourteenth Amendment claims and providing that such claims shall receive final enforcement in the state courts. As the Court noted in *Katzenbach v. Morgan* (1966), 'section 5 is a positive grant of legislative power authorizing Congress to exercise its discretion in determining whether and what legislation is needed to secure the guarantees of the Fourteenth Amendment.' It is certainly within the broad scope of #5 for Congress to determine that in certain cases, such as abortion and school desegregation cases, the grants of due process and equal protection are more appropriately enforced by state courts."

Explaining further, Roberts wrote: "The history of the Fourteenth Amendment strongly supports the authority of Congress to advance its view of the appropriate means of enforcing the guarantees of due process and equal protection under #5. The Fourteenth Amendment was drafted and passed in an atmosphere of great hostility to the Supreme Court. . . .[Congress] had suffered great defeats at the hands of the High Court in the *Dred Scott* and *Fugitive Slave* decisions. A court which would render such decisions was certainly not to be entrusted with securing the protections of the Thirteenth through Fifteenth Amendments. In the view of the Framers of the Civil War Amendments, therefore, Congress was to have primary responsibility for providing for the enforcement of the guarantees of due process and equal protection. . . . It is of course true that the Supreme Court has long since assumed a dominant role in enforcing the Fourteenth Amendment. This does not, however, detract from the authority of Congress to enter the field under section 5 as originally contemplated." Roberts Memorandum, "Prospects to Divest the Supreme Court of Appellate Jurisdiction: An Analysis in Light of Recent Developments" (undated), 25-26. See also, Austin Bramwell, "Pleading the Fourteenth," *The American Conservative*, Jan. 31, 2005, 13.

- Congress used its Article III power in 2005 to order completion of a fence on our southern border near San Diego which had been held up for ten years by environmental lawsuits. By the REAL ID Act, Congress legislated that the fence should go forward with "expeditious construction" and that "no court... shall have jurisdiction to hear any cause or claim" to stop it. This law has already been upheld as constitutional by a federal court.

- The GAO study, released in 1997, found 1,049 federal statutory provisions in the United States Code, as of the date DOMA was signed into law, in which benefits, rights and privileges are contingent on marital status or in which marital status is a factor. Subsequently, the GAO identified 120 statutory provisions involving marital status that were enacted between Sept. 21, 1996 and Dec. 31, 2003, and 31 provisions that were repealed or amended to eliminate marital status as a factor. Consequently as of Dec. 31, 2003, the revised GAO total of federal statutory provisions in which marital status is a factor is 1,138.

• The Supreme Court affirmed a provision of the Ohio constitution requiring near-unanimity by its supreme court before reversing a lower court and invalidating a statute as unconstitutional (*Ohio ex rel. Bryant v. Akron Metropolitan Park District*, 1930).

• Ninth Circuit Federal Judge Stephen Reinhardt, appointed by Jimmy Carter in 1980, is probably the most supremacist judge in America. His opinion in *Fields v. Palmdale* (2005) asserting that parents have no rights in public schools is only the latest example of his sweeping liberal decisions. In *Silveira v. Lockyer* (2002), his seventy-page opinion discussed the Second Amendment at length and asserted that there is no individual right to keep and bear arms, citing with approval the bogus research of Michael Bellesiles. (Reinhardt later issued an amended opinion omitting the references to Bellesiles.) Reinhardt is married to Ramona Ripston, who has been executive director of the ACLU of Southern California since 1972, was a co-founder of NARAL in 1969, a leader in People for the American Way, and a longtime political associate and appointee of Los Angeles Mayor Villaraigosa. Ripston was responsible for forcing Los Angeles County to remove the tiny cross from its seal, and she led the initial court victory attempting to stop the 2003 recall of Governor Gray Davis based on a phony argument about voting machines (which the full Ninth Circuit reversed). Ripston is Reinhardt's third wife and he is her fifth husband.

• Sarasota Circuit Court Judge Harry Rapkin was properly criticized for his handling of the probation of Joseph P. Smith, who was charged in the death of eleven-year-old Carlie Brucia. *Sarasota Herald Tribune*, April 23, 2004.

• For an example of a nineteen-year-old consent decree, see the Notes for Chapter 2 re: Judge Myron Thompson.

- The law that authorizes attorney's fees to the ACLU and others for anti-God lawsuits was passed by the Watergate Congress in 1976 under the name "Civil Rights Attorney's Fees Awards Act." It is codified as 42 U.S.C. Section 1988(b). Congress should repeal or amend it so that attorney's fees are not allowed in lawsuits claiming a violation of the Establishment Clause.

- For the Redlands controversy, see the Associated Press or *Los Angeles Times*, April 29, 2004, B1.

- This 1996 law review article documents how scholars have shifted toward the individual rights interpretation of the Second Amendment. It says that only three out of thirty-four law review articles written since 1980 oppose the individual rights interpretation, and two of those were written by anti-gun lobbyists. "Toward a Functional Framework for Interpreting the Second Amendment" by Scott Bursor, 74 *Texas Law Review* 1125-1151 (1996).

- The quotation from Thomas Jefferson is from his letter to Charles Hammond in 1821.

- For the Supreme Court justices discussing *Mellen v. Bunting* in eight conferences, see the article by Linda Greenhouse, *New York Times*, April 27, 2004, A22.

- In October 2005, a survey released by the *ABA Journal eReport* reported that a majority of Americans agree with the statements that "judicial activism" has reached "a crisis," that judges "ignore traditional morality," that judges are "arrogant, out-of-control and unaccountable," and that judges who ignore voters' values "should be impeached." This was a random-sample poll of the general population made by Opinion Research Corporation and commissioned by the American Bar Association. The lawyers who ordered the survey were in shock at the results.

Web links and updates are available online at
www.Schlafly.net/judges/

Index

abortion: Constitution, U. S. and, 85; partial-birth, 87; as "right", 5, 9; *stare decisis* and, 86–87; states and, 84

acknowledgment of God: Bible and, 34–35; Christmas and, 34, 35; Congress and, 169–71; crosses and seals and, 33–35; Declaration of Independence and, 17; First Amendment and, 17–18, 20–21, 25, 26, 30–31, 32, 36, 38, 169, 170, 189; judicial censoring of, 16–38; military and, 16; Pledge of Allegiance and, 4, 12, 16, 17–23, 170, 176, 189; prayer in public schools and, 21–22, 29–32, 176; Ten Commandments and, 4, 16, 21, 23–29, 93, 170, 182–84. *See also* religion

Adams, John, 40, 65, 142

Afroyim, Beys, 111–12

Alabama: capital punishment and, 57; franchising felons and, 122; prayer in schools and, 31; property rights and, 72; Ten Commandments in, 24–26, 182–84

Alaska, 39, 49

Alexander, Lamar, 181

Alito, Samuel, 156, 159

Allen Douglas W., 226

America. *See* United States

American Bar Association (ABA), 149–51, 235

American Civil Liberties Union (ACLU): acknowledgment of God and, 20, 189; attorney's fees and, 182–83; Boy Scouts and, 35–36; California recall and, 118–19; crosses and seals and, 33–34; feminization of judiciary and, 88; franchising felons and, 122, 124;

Pledge of Allegiance and, 19; pornography and, 78; same-sex marriage and, 43; Ten Commandments and, 24, 25, 27, 29

American Constitution Society, 60

American Dream, 68

American Indians, 107–8

American Revolution, 171

Americans United for Separation of Church and State, 24, 29, 183

Amnesty International, 105

Arizona, 5, 57, 92, 107, 141

Arkansas, 5, 57

Ashcroft, John, 187

assisted suicide, 173–74

Associated Press, 121

atheism, atheists: acknowledgment of God and, 14, 16, 20, 21; crosses and, 33; prayer in schools and, 31; Ten Commandments and, 26, 27

attorney's fees, 183–85

236

Index

Pomona, 33–34
pornography, 14; First
    Amendment and,
    73–74, 76–80, 82–83;
    on Internet, 79–80;
    judicial promotion of,
    73–83; military and,
    78; movies and, 73, 77;
    in prisons, 81–82; as
    "right", 5; social value
    and, 74–75; Warren,
    Earl and. *see* pornog-
    raphy
Portal-to-Portal Act of
    1947, 164
prayer, in public schools,
    21–22, 29–32, 176
President: acknowledg-
    ment of God and,
    16–17; judicial su-
    premacy and, 12–14
prisons: judicial micro-
    management of, 6,
    179–82; pornography
    in, 81–82; women in, 89
private property. *See*
    property rights
profanity. *See* pornog-
    raphy
property rights, 56;
    Constitution, U. S.,
    rewriting of, and,
    70–72; eminent domain
    and, 64, 69; judicial
    threatening of, 64–72;
    public use and, 64–66,
    70; Warren Court and,
    66–69
public schools: immigra-
    tion and, 105–7; judicial
    interference in, 105–7;
    judicial micromanage-
    ment of, 6, 179–82;
    judicial taxation and,
    137–41; Pledge of Al-
    legiance in, 4, 16, 17–23,
    170; Ten Command-
    ments in, 21

racial preferences: college

admissions and, 5, 55;
    employment and, 5
Raleigh, Sir Walter, 37
Reagan, Ronald, 25, 92
Rehnquist, William,
    166; abortion and, 85;
    Election 2000 and,
    117; immigration and,
    102; judicial taxation
    and, 133–35; Pledge of
    Allegiance and, 18, 23;
    religion and, 32
Reinhardt, Stephen, 59,
    60, 234
religion: definition of, 26;
    establishment of, 18,
    20–21, 26, 30–31, 170;
    First Amendment and,
    26; free exercise of, 18,
    170; judicial prejudice
    against, 13, 22; in public
    life, 18. *See also* ac-
    knowledgment of God
Rembar, Charles, 74
Reno, Janet, 59
rights: Declaration of
    Independence and, 20;
    homosexual, 43–46,
    58–59, 60; parental,
    125–32; property,
    56, 64–72; same-sex
    marriage and, 46–49;
    substantive, 9–10; vot-
    ing, 59, 121–24
Roberts, John G., 63, 166
Roberts, Owen J., 166
Robinson, Mary, 53
Rockefeller, Nelson, 84
Roosevelt, Franklin D., 13
Roosevelt, Theodore, 35
Rothstein, Barbara J., 173
rule of law, x, 10, 15, 93–94
Rutgers Law School, 124
Ryan, James E., 140–41

Salt Lake City, Utah, 28
same-sex marriage: as
    civil rights issue,
    46–49; Congress and,
    167–69; Constitution,

U. S. and, 42; First
    Amendment and, 50;
    international law and,
    58–59; marriage, redefi-
    nition of, and, 39–43;
    in Massachusetts, 11,
    40–43; as "right", 5
San Salvador, 34
Saudi Arabia, 57
Scalia, Antonin: ac-
    knowledgment of God
    and, 37–38; capital
    punishment and, 97,
    99; Constitution,
    U. S., as living and
    evolving and, 11, 12;
    Election 2000 and,
    117; homosexual rights
    and, 44–45; interna-
    tional law and, 54, 56,
    58; judicial supremacy
    and, 15, 148–49; judicial
    taxation and, 133–35;
    morals legislation and,
    82; prayer in schools
    and, 31; Ten Com-
    mandments and, 37–38
Schwarzenegger, Arnold,
    119
Scott, Dred, 144–47
seals, 33–35
Second Amendment, 186
Second Circuit U. S.
    Court of Appeals, 78
secular humanism, 32
self-government:
    Congress and, 172–74;
    freedom and, 6; judi-
    cial supremacy and, 15;
    restoration of, 158–91;
    right to, 114–15; in
    United States, ix
Senate, U. S.. *See* Con-
    gress
Sensenbrenner, F. James,
    Jr., 100–101, 171–72
Sex Bias in the U. S. Code
    (Ginsburg), 88, 90
Simmons, Christopher,
    98–99

Acknowledgment

Phyllis Schlafly acknowledges the assistance of her son Roger, who contributed his skill of logic to the analysis of the complex court decisions in this book and their relation to the unconstitutional doctrine of judicial supremacy. Roger has a BSE from Princeton University, a PHD in mathematics from the University of California Berkeley, and a license to practice patent law before the United States Patent and Trademark Office.

Phyllis Schlafly received her J.D. from Washington University Law School and is admitted to the practice of law in Missouri, Illinois, the District of Columbia, and the U.S. Supreme Court. She holds a master's degree in government from Harvard University.

Mrs. Schlafly served as a member of the Commission on the Bicentennial of the U.S. Constitution, 1985-1991, appointed by President Reagan and chaired by Chief Justice Warren Burger. She served four years on the Administrative Conference of the United States and ten years on the Illinois Commission on the Status of Women. She has testified before more than fifty congressional and state legislative committees on constitutional, education, strategic defense, foreign policy, electronic privacy, and family issues.

A prolific writer, Mrs. Schlafly is the author or editor of twenty books on subjects as varied as politics (*A Choice Not An Echo*), family and feminism (*Feminist Fantasies* and *The Power of the Positive Woman*), nuclear strategy (*Strike From Space* and *Kissinger on the Couch*), education (*Child Abuse in the Classroom*), child care (*Who Will Rock the Cradle?*), and reading (*Turbo Reader*).

Mrs. Schlafly has written her newsletter, *The Phyllis Schlafly Report*, monthly since 1967. Her syndicated newspaper column, which she has written since 1977, appears in one hundred newspapers. Her radio commentaries, aired since 1983, are heard daily on 460 stations, and she has conducted a call-in talk show on education, heard on forty-five stations, since 1989. Phyllis Schlafly was named one of the one hundred most important women of the twentieth century by the *Ladies' Home Journal*. She has appeared on virtually every national television and radio talk show and has lectured or debated on more than five hundred college and university campuses.

Named the Illinois Mother of the Year in 1992, Mrs. Schlafly is the mother of six children: three attorneys, one orthopedic surgeon, one mathematician, and one businesswoman; and she has fourteen grandchildren.

This book was designed and set into type

by Mitchell S. Muncy,

with a cover design by Stephen J. Ott,

and printed and bound

by Bang Printing,

Brianerd, Minnesota.

❧

The text face is Caslon,

designed by Carol Twombly,

based on faces cut by William Caslon, London, in the 1730s

and issued in digital form by Adobe Systems,

Mountain View, California, in 1989.

❧   OSMA Ben laden

The paper is acid-free and is of archival quality.

John ROBevts
John PAUl stevens —
38
ANTONIN SCALA
ANTHONY KENNEDY —
DAVID SoulTER —
CLARENCE THOMAS
RUTH BADER GINSBURG
Steven BREVER —
SAMuel ALITO